AMALGAMATION

PONTYPRIDD RFC
AT TAFF VALE PARK
- THE EARLY DAYS

AMALGAMATION

PONTYPRIDD RFC
AT TAFF VALE PARK
- THE EARLY DAYS

By

Gareth Harris

First Published in Great Britain in
September 1999

Published by:
Coalopolis Publishing
9 Cefn Lane, Glyncoch, Pontypridd CF37 3BP

© Coalopolis Publishing 1999

Printed by:
ProPrint
Riverside Cottage
Great North Road
Stibbington
Peterborough PE8 6LR

British Library Cataloguing-in-publication Data

A catalogue record of this book is available from the British Library

ISBN: 0 9536475 0 1

CONTENTS:

ILLUSTRATIONS

About The Author

Gareth Harris is Pontypridd born and bred, and has always had a healthy interest in local history. In his school days in the early 1960s he would sneak into the rugby ground at Ynysangharad Park to watch Pontypridd RFC play. As a teenager he was an all round sportsman; a talented soccer player, and also played rugby for the Pontypridd schools rugby team. When his playing career concluded, he took up refereeing in the local soccer leagues. It was during this period that he started going to watch Pontypridd RFC games at Sardis Road, and around 1977 eventually gave up refereeing to watch rugby.

His interest in the club's history was sparked after hearing that a player had died playing for the team, and after a little research he shared what he discovered by writing an article in a match programme in 1995. There was so much that he discovered about the club that he started writing regularly in the club programme, and continues to do so today. After two seasons he decided to pool his information into a book, 'THE BUTCHERS ARMS BOYS', published by Rugby Unlimited in 1997. The success of this book encouraged Gareth, who knew that the era between 1890 and 1893 was a particularly interesting period, to complete a follow up book entitled 'AMALGAMATION.' Despite initial rejection by a publisher, he persevered until the curator of The Pontypridd Historical Centre, Brian Davies, renewed Gareth's enthusiasm and the end result is the publication of this book.

FOREWORD

BY PETER JOHNSON OF BBC RADIO WALES

The exploits of Pontypridd RFC in the modern era have put the town firmly on the world rugby map. The playing record of the last decade or so speaks for itself. "Ponty" has become a byword for entertaining rugby in a warm and family-friendly atmosphere. But how many of the thousands who flock to Sardis Road know the incredible story of the journey from the weekly struggle to raise a side in the 1870s to the House Of Pain of the 1990s? Thanks to "The Butchers Arms Boys" and the hard work and enthusiasm of its author, many more people are now acquainted with the like of Ack Llewellin and Ben Tiley, heroes of another era. And what an era it was!

Rugby football was young and vibrant. It was finding a place in the heart of Welsh working people. The game was putting down roots in the booming capital of the coalfield. In this, his second volume, Gareth Harris describes a period of amalgamation and consolidation. "Football" as they called it was becoming part of the town landscape, yet the game was still novel enough for those who reported it in the fiercely competitive local press to be less than certain about what was happening on the pitch.

The rivalries traced in this book and the chaotic, even shambolic nature of the organisation of the game will raise many a smile. Disarray in Welsh rugby is not an exclusively modern phenomenon. Gareth deserves the thanks of fans old and new who may have been tempted to assume the history of Ponty rugby has been one long success story. It hasn't. His continuing hard work brings us a tale dotted with colour, character and courage. I think I would have enjoyed a night with Teddy Lewis at a Smoker at the Sportsman Hotel. I am sure you will enjoy reading about it too.

PETER JOHNSON,
PONTYPRIDD,
MARCH 1999

INTRODUCTION (1)

BY THE AUTHOR

This is the second in a series of books recording the early days of Pontypridd RFC. My first book in conjunction with Alun Evans, "The Butchers Arms Boys" (Published by Rugby Unlimited - 1997) chronicled the formation of the club, its early success, through to its demise around Christmas 1888.

This new book continues by charting its rebirth and ultimate rise into the higher echelons of "Football" in the principality. During this period, what remained of the Pontypridd club forged an amalgamation with the Treforest club, and set about building a field and stadium at the Taff Vale grounds that would be equal to most in the country. There were also famous victories over Cardiff and Swansea; the death of a player; another amalgamation; and a colliery disaster that forced the prolonging of one season.

The scoring system at this period was a little complicated, with point scoring not officially introduced until the 1892-93 season, but I have tried to give some indication of the score by giving the equivalent score in italics. A 'Goal' was a converted try. Where possible I have written match reports as they appeared in the newspapers of the time.

In my search for information, several people and organisations have been of great help to me, especially the staff of the Pontypridd Public Library. I would also like to thank the Pontypridd Historical Centre, The

Glamorgan Record Office, Cardiff Central Library, Llanelli, Swansea, Treorchy, Merthyr and Aberdare Public Libraries.

Many thanks to Peter Johnson, the eminent broadcaster, and Brian Davies, curator of the Pontypridd Historical Centre for their kind introductions. Without the help and encouragement of Mr Davies, Ann Cleary and David Gwyer, this book would never have been completed, and I am eternally grateful for their support.

Thanks also to my wife Elaine, who had to put up with me being AWOL doing research over several years.

GARETH HARRIS
JULY 1999

INTRODUCTION (2)

BY BRIAN DAVIES
CURATOR OF PONTYPRIDD
HISTORICAL CENTRE

Pontypridd is unlike most of the larger valley towns. There was no village here before the chainworks and even after the first half century of its industrial era Pontypridd was still a small town. But in the thirty years before the First World War Pontypridd grew at an explosive rate.

Jack Jones, the novelist, made Pontypridd in its 'Klondike' years the backdrop for his novel "Some Trust in Chariots." In 1890 it was then the centre of the most important coalfield in Britain; a town of 40,000, with its thriving market just completed. A lively place for theatre and boxing, *"as sporting as it is musical and religious and drunken to about the same degree"*.

Jack only got one thing wrong. He wrote about Pontypridd as if its people were all Welsh, when most of them were anything but. One minister who came to preach at the Tabernacle church was warned by his Rhondda congregation that he was going to *"a very English place"*. This was also an oversimplification. Pontypridd was a patchwork of nationalities. At the beginning of the twentieth century the only part of Pontypridd Urban District where a sizeable proportion of the population spoke Welsh was Cilfynydd. In Treforest and Hopkinstown there were many Irish. Trallwn was so cosmopolitan that one local councillor joked that the most appropriate language for a public meeting there would be Esperanto. The Graig was solidly Yorkshire. The miners' lodges in these early years reflected the origins of their members, two of them being affiliated to the local Welsh miners' union while the other two, including Maritime, joined the English miners union.

Yet just as the miners set aside differences of nationality when they came together to form a single union, so the eventual creation of a united Pontypridd rugby team was a significant milestone in the transformation of a raw and new town into a community with a distinct sense of its own identity. Gareth Harris has done a service for the club and for the town, in writing this book. I am sure that we all look forward to the next volume.

BRIAN DAVIES
APRIL 1999

This book is dedicated to my son Carl,
whom life has dealt a poor hand,
and who I love most dearly

CHAPTER ONE

REBIRTH OF THE PONTYPRIDD FOOTBALL CLUB - FIRST DAYS AT TAFF VALE PARK

When the first Pontypridd Football Club folded around Christmas 1888 and some of its players started playing for the Treforest team, it looked like the final curtain for the "club" founded around 1877-78 by James Spickett at the Glamorgan County Courthouse in Pontypridd, but one man, Edward Llewellin, a former club captain from the mid 1880s, was determined to resurrect it in a very short period. He believed that the new club should this time be for the working class people of the district, and not as before, when it was practically a private club for the middle class young men of the town.

With the assistance of another ex-player, his brother Alfred (known to everyone as "Ack") Edward started to plan a team for the 1890-91 season. They believed that there would be no problems in getting players, as some ex-Pontypridd players were still without a team and others, playing for Treforest, had intimated that the two clubs could amalgamate, but Edwards' biggest problem was finding a field to play on. The previous club had played at the Ynysangharad grounds, near the town centre, but had relied upon tenants of the fields or the goodwill of the Newbridge Chainworks manager, Mr Gordon Lenox, who looked after the grounds of the Llanover Estate, for somewhere to play. Edward eventually contacted Mr James Roberts of Forest House, Treforest, a local councillor, and manager of the Forest Iron Works, which was in sad decline. Mr Roberts was a keen follower of all sports and came to a financial agreement with Edward Llewellin for the use of land alongside the river Taff to lay out a field and construct a stadium. The amount was undisclosed.

Meanwhile, as the old Pontypridd club had come to an end another team had taken the mantle of the town's "premier" team, namely, the Maritime Colliery team. It was composed of one or two ex-Pontypridd players, but mainly men from the North of England, who had arrived with the manager of the new pit, who had promised them work. Whether the old Pontypridd team still existed at the time of the birth of the Maritime team was debatable, but what is evident is that between 1888 and 1890, the colliery team had steadily improved their fixture list and had achieved increasing success. Their pack, consisting of men who were used to manual labour, was a match for any other eight. They initially played on the People's Park, Mill Street, near the town centre, but then moved on to play on a field in Maesycoed, which was the property of the colliery. With the planned reformation of the Pontypridd team, would there be room for two "Premier" teams in the town?

The First AGM

Edward Llewellin called a general meeting of The Pontypridd Football Club (probably the first) for Friday, August 8th 1890, at the Sportsman Hotel, Pontypridd, when over seventy of the leading players of the district attended. Mr Abrahamson of Treforest presided, and throughout proceedings were most unanimous and enthusiastic, which augured well for the success of the new club. The secretary, Mr Edward Llewellin, announced that councillor Roberts, the president of the club, had given consent to improvements being carried out by the club, which would make the ground one of the best in Wales, and that the committee intended to erect a grandstand. Edward had done a remarkable job securing games, and announced that home and away fixtures had been arranged with most of the leading clubs in South Wales including: Cardiff, Llanelly, Neath, Aberavon, Penarth, Penygraig, Cardiff Harlequins, Pontymister and Caerphilly, and was also arranging with other good teams to fill the vacant dates. He further announced that arrangements were being made for a match on Christmas Day with the celebrated London Welsh team and that he was corresponding with several Northern teams. In this historic meeting, these people were elected to the following posts:

First Team Captain: Ack Llewellin
Vice Captain: Francis Miles
Second Team Captain: Reuben Richards
Vice Captain: Tom Evans
Thursday First Team Captain: W J Davies
Vice Captain: Gwilym Morgan
Second Thursday Team Captain: C Arnott
Vice Captain: Dan Evans
Secretary: Edward Llewellin
Treasurer: Evan Williams
President: James Roberts
Assistant Secretaries: Ivor Howell
and J Marshall

Mr James Roberts JP
Benefactor to the Pontypridd Football Club

In 1878 James Roberts became the manager of the Forest Iron and Steel Works Co until they closed fourteen years later. He became a member of the Glamorgan County Council, Chairman of the Pontypridd Burial Board and the County School of Governors and various other committees. He always associated himself energetically with the political, social and religious movements in the district. Throughout his life he was an ardent advocate for the best educational facilities for the people and always tried to impress upon the young the need for them to make best use of their school years. If he had a hobby it may be said that it was working for the education of the children. In 1890 he allowed the reconstituted Pontypridd Football Club to rent his company's land in Treforest so that they could build a stadium that would later become known as Taff Vale Park. Pontypridd played there from 1890 to 1901. James Roberts was

President of Pontypridd RFC in seasons 1890-91, 91-92 and 93-94.

Preparation For Season

From August 30th 1890, a series of practice matches were held at "Miles's Field", Treforest, the players changing across the river at the Llanbradach Arms, alongside the Glamorganshire canal, players being requested to turn up on the Saturday at 3 o'clock sharp. The season would commence with an away match against the celebrated Llanelly team, and it was thought essential that intending members should take every opportunity to get into form.

The Taff Vale Grounds

In early September 1890, the Western Mail carried this report about Pontypridd's new ground:

'The field, which is snugly enclosed, lies just off the tramroad at Treforest and has been levelled and titivated at considerable expense. On the tramroad side at Treforest a substantial grandstand has been erected and Pontypridd can now boast of a ground which would not discredit a far more pretentious locality. Close upon £100 has been spent - and well spent - during the last summer on improvements, so that matches can be played under pleasant conditions. An entrance to the field from the tramroad has lessened the distance from Pontypridd by exactly half. Five hundred cartloads of an adjoining tip has been removed to enlarge and level the ground and this, with the spacious new pavilion, ought to result in a substantial addition to the gate money. Councillor

James Roberts, the owner of the ground has given the club most generous assistance and thanks to this and the indomitable energy of Mr Edward Llewellin, the honorary secretary, the public of Pontypridd and the neighbouring towns may soon have to learn to take intelligent and kindly interest in football and athletics in general.'

The Season Begins

The reconstituted Pontypridd club began its new career with a visit to Stradey Park, Llanelly, on September 20th 1890, when they ran out in their resplendent new red and white jerseys and they quite surprised the Llanelly folk who had gathered to watch the opening match of the season and were only defeated by three tries to nil (3-0). One Llanelly newspaper showed how Pontypridd had earned respect during the match. They wrote:

'The visitors, who the "Tinplaters" were inclined to view from the heights of superiority, played a rattling good game and with patience and painstaking practice they ought to do well this season.'

PONTYPRIDD FOOTBALL CLUB
Fixture Card 1890-91

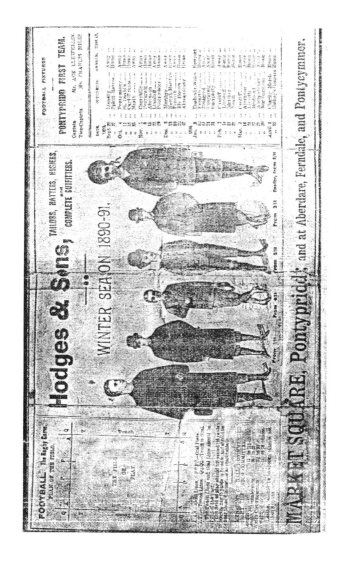

The Pontypridd team that played in this historic fixture was:

Fullback, Ben Lewis; Threequarters, Alf Lewis, Noah Morgan, J Appleby, J W Cooper; Halves, George Gould and Tom Evans; Forwards, Ack Llewellin (C), Francis Miles, Bill Williams, G Thorne, J Nicholas, J Edwards, Ivor Howells and J Evans.

The First Home Game

The following Saturday, Pontypridd secured a creditable draw at Pontymister, the Monmouthshire cup holders, by a drop goal each (3-3).

At last, on September 27th 1890, Pontypridd played their first match at their new field at the Taff Vale Grounds and started a new period in the club's history with a three try to one (3-1) victory over Splott Rovers. The team that played in this historic match showed several changes from that which played against Llanelly and Pontymister and was:

Fullback, Ben Lewis; Threequarters, J Appleby, Alun Morgan, Reuben Richards, Alf Lewis; Halves, George Gould, Christmas Jones; Forwards, Ack Llewellin (C), Francis Miles, Bill Williams, J Nicholas, G Thorne, Ivor Howells, J Evans and J Edwards

The Western Mail commented:

'Pontypridd were in splendid form, and sanguine expectations are locally entertained that they will soon force their way to the front rank in South Wales. There is reason to believe that because of the recent

amalgamation of the Treforest and Pontypridd clubs, that old sores of the past have now been completely healed, with the result that the weakening of efforts of an injudicious division of forces will, it is hoped, be felt no more. The team now consists of the pick of the whole district, and with a little more training the few blemishes that characterised their display against Splott, will disappear.'

Pontypridd suffered mixed results over the next few weeks, including a heavy six tries to nil defeat at Neath. Off the field the club had problems as well. A Brake was supplied by ex-Pontypridd player Edwin Phillips, of the Lamb and Flag Hotel, for an away fixture in Caerphilly on November 1st 1890, but it appears to have broken down, and a local newspaper reported that *"a stiff walk occupied the greater portion of their time"*. No doubt the Brake supplied failed to climb the Nantgarw Hill!

Big Crowd for Local Derby

Amidst the greatest excitement ever known in connection with a football context in Pontypridd, Penygraig visited the Taff Vale Ground on November 8th 1890. This encounter brought together devotees to the number of several hundreds from the Rhondda valley and altogether some 2,000 spectators attended. The contest had formed the engrossing topic of conversation of football enthusiasts right through the valleys for some time.

The excitement on the field was intense and it turned out to be the most exciting game seen at the ground so far. Considering the history of the Penygraig team over the last five seasons, and especially their good record over the last two seasons, when they even defeated the famous Leeds team, Pontypridd's display was praiseworthy in the extreme. Penygraig was not fully represented, but they still fielded a formidable team. It was feared by the admirers of Pontypridd that the visitors had come down determined to win, but the plucky way in which the home team met every attack of their opponents, surprised everybody. The opinion ventured was that in none of their previous matches had Pontypridd exhibited such splendid form, and a try by Nicholas, converted by George Harry, secured them a fine draw with one goal each (3-3).

A Bitter Defeat

The following week Pontypridd followed up their excellent display against Penygraig with an equally fine display by defeating Aberavon at Home. On November 22nd 1890, Pontypridd travelled to play another big game against Llandaff in Cardiff. The Pontypridd Chronicle reported:

'With such a record as the city boys are able to boast, it is not surprising that our representatives went down to Llandaff with not even sanguine expectations. The Pontypridd men arrived by the two o'clock train and proceeded a distance of about half a mile to the Malsters Arms, where they put up. Both teams trotted out their best men, and if anything, betting ruled in favour of the home men, who were, from reports, determined to show Penygraig that they could "whop" a team that Penygraig could only draw with. A goodly sprinkling of spectators line the ropes.'

As it turned out, Llandaff did show Penygraig a thing or two, and triumphed by one goal and three tries to nil (0-6), Pontypridd doing well until injuries and the retirement of winger Alf Lewis with a strained neck, contributed to a certain extent to the heavy defeat.

A Social Event

During the first week of December 1890, the second in a series of smoking concerts given by the Pontypridd Football Club, took place at the Sportsman Hotel. Mr Teddy Lewis occupied the chair and in opening the proceedings treated the audience to a splendid oration, bristling throughout with those brilliant passages from his own dictation for which he was notorious. The singing was of a mediocre character until the star (?) of the evening, arrayed in his regimentals, and with the letters TVR (Taff Vale Railway) figuring on his cap, was called upon. Directly this artiste struck up his keynote, the first thought that crossed everyone's mind was that Simms Reeves (a singing star of the musical hall at this period) had arrived. And not only could he sing, but was actually warbling the sweet music of the well known song "Soon we shall be in London town". Could people be dreaming? No, it was he - but as he really got going, everyone wished he really was in London town!

At the end of the evening a vote of thanks to the chairman having been proposed and seconded, Mr Lewis rose amidst the cheering of the assembled "thousands" to reply, and as he stood at the head of the table and boldly and earnestly advocated the claims of the Pontypridd team to a place in the front rank, one could not help but admire the man. A vote of thanks to Mr D E Phillips for his presence on the piano having been passed, a very enjoyable evening was brought to a close by the singing of "God bless the Prince of Wales".

Spectators Employed in Game

On December 6th 1890, Pontypridd visited Merthyr and fielded six of the second team, but had things practically all their own way throughout. Merthyr were wretchedly represented, though a full team still might have availed nothing. Only nine of the men selected on the home team turned up, and recourse had to be had by the employment of what was described as "as scratchy lot of substitutes" chosen from intending spectators around the field - which, it was commented "is situated over a mile from the town". Although the match was timed for a three o'clock kick off, the ball was not set rolling until quarter to four, so that it was quite dark before the game finished. Pontypridd secured an easy victory by three goals to two tries to one try (11-1), largely due to halfback, Ben Tiley, who despite being "hors-de-combat" for awhile in the second half, returned to add another goal to the two he had recorded earlier.

A Look At The Future

The same day that Pontypridd faced Merthyr, the Pontypridd Herald previewed the Maritime Colliery team's visit to Neath the following weekend. It wrote:

'On Saturday next, the Maritime team journey to do battle with the doughty exponents of the winter pastime, Neath, who it is well known, have this season

under the captaincy of "the Doctor", fought their way into the front rank, and are fairly entitled to be classed amongst the few first class clubs of South Wales. The Maritime team have also played well this season, and it is to be hoped that they will uphold their reputation. This becomes all the more wishful from the fact that Neath literally sat on Pontypridd when the "Red and White" lads visited them, and I for one, should greatly rejoice to see the defeat of our town team avenged. But why it is that a fixture cannot be arranged between Maritime and Pontypridd? The match, were it to come about, would no doubt result in the biggest gate ever seen in Pontypridd.'

The following weekend, the Maritime put up a much better show than Pontypridd when they were only defeated by one try to nil (1-0). The Maritime team that day included J Appleby, who had played for Pontypridd at the start of the season. Had pressure been brought upon him by his employers to play for the Colliery team? However, the Maritime team that day would become the basis of the Pontypridd team of the future and was:

Fullback, Walter Gay; Threequarters, Jack Murray, Ben Dickenson, S O Else, J Appleby; Halves, Steve Sullivan (C) and Tudor Foster; Forwards, Hope, Tom Murray, Harry Stead, Patsy Devereaux, Tom Hemsworth, Spencer, Jimmy Connelly. Reserves, Leech, Lewis and Tom Hope.

Disgrace At Mountain Ash

Games in this period were often rough and sometimes dirty, however, occasionally there were games better off forgotten, and when Pontypridd visited Mountain Ash on

December 11th 1890, this became one of them. The Glamorgan Free Press reported:

'This was the first, and what a lot of people hoped was the last time that Pontypridd would visit Mountain Ash. The game, if it could be called that, ended in victory for the homesters by a goal and drop goal, to a goal and a try (6-4), but they were not worthy of the name "footballers", and if all their visitors are treated as Pontypridd were, then next season they will have to play with themselves, for certain it is that they will get no teams to visit them a second time. An old saying and one which is especially applicable in this case is "Once bitten - twice shy". Not only were the Mountain Ash men exceedingly rough, but, to make a long story short, a more dirty foul mounted lot of ruffians could never be met! The game, as long as football was being played was altogether in favour of the visitors, who scored a try in the first twenty minutes of play against a very strong wind. After that, however, the homesters recognised the fact that they were simply not in it, and resorted to "horse play", which, together with language that to hear was enough to make one's blood run cold, enabled them to pull the match out of the fire. But the drop goal that they were credited with was no goal at all, the ball passing quite six inches under the crossbar, thus securing a win for Mountain Ash by one point. To have some idea of the referee's impartiality (?), it was noticed that he once clapped the home team after seeing them sprint ten yards!'

Reserves Battle Hard

Pontypridd's home fixture against Newport Harriers on December 13th 1890, was postponed due to the weather, but the reserves, however, not having played for three long weeks, were not to be deterred even by such a severe visitation of frost. In their match against Cogan, they found their opponents composed of half of the St David's first team, whose game at Penygraig had also been postponed, but it was the first opportunity that captain Teddy Lewis had of showing what fine fettle the Pontypridd reserves were in, and there was no denying the "young ones" were game too, as with a score of one goal and two tries against them at half time, they made a draw of it, a fact that speaks volumes for their superior staying powers. The Glamorgan Free Press was critical of the club selection committee and wrote:

'At threequarter, George Harry played a good game, and the try he scored was obtained in the coolest manner possible. And now a word about Mr Harry. It is said that the committee intend passing him by, or in other words, chucking him out. They must ask themselves first of all if they have another good enough to replace him. Certain it is that were they to take this step, they will be sacrificing the fastest man in the team.'

The Big Freeze

After the postponement of the Newport Harriers game, snow and frost took its toll on the Pontypridd fixture list, which caused some criticism of the match committee from some quarters. The Pontypridd Herald of January 17th 1891 commented:

*'Football in Pontypridd is a dead letter, and has
been for the last few weeks, and is likely to continue until
"Mr Frost" once more yields up possession of the field,
which at the moment appears more like a skating rink
than a football field. This state of things prevailed again
on Saturday and the Pontypridd committee, not having a
particular desire to call upon the funds of the insurance
company, very wisely decided to cry off the match with
Penarth. But still, I imagine that if the committee of the
"Red and Whites" had taken steps to clear the ground
after the fall of snow which was experienced during
Christmas week, the match and those against
Abergavenny, Ely Rovers and the Cardiff District and
the 'A' team fixtures as well, could have been brought
off. Still, it is no good crying over spilt milk and the loss
which their "penny wise - pound foolish" policy, has
entailed upon their own heads. But here I am wrong, I
should have said "greatest loss", for surely season ticket
holders are entitled to a voice on the matter, and I
question if any one of them would have become such if
they had known the circumstances which now prevail.'*

A False Restart

At last, on January 24th 1891, Pontypridd got back on
the playing field for a match at Penygraig. Unfortunately,
the match at the Belle Vue ground did not last long. The
soil was a perfect quagmire, and rain fell in torrents and
a strong wind was blowing. After fifteen minutes play
the rain increased and the fury of the gale got stronger.
The players, apparently with one accord, agreed to
abandon operations and they unanimously raced up the
field and out of the enclosure. The spectators were not

disappointed, for most of them wondered that the contest had begun at all. A rush was made for the gate, the spectators claiming the refunding of their money. The home secretary, however, declined, but presented each applicant with a ticket of admission for some future occasion.

Home Fixture At Last

On January 31st 1891, after six long weeks of patient waiting, the local spectators were treated to some first team football when Pontypridd defeated Caerphilly at Taff Vale Park by two goals and three tries to nil (9-0). Despite this good victory, there was still talk of an amalgamation. The Pontypridd Chronicle commented:

'If the game signified one thing, it was that Pontypridd are capable of doing strong things. It has, I think, been very well said that Pontypridd has the makings of a good representative team, and Saturday's form proved this beyond doubt. I believe that the proposal has gone forth to the great multitude of local enthusiasts that the affiliated teams of Pontypridd and Maritime would gain the front. Whatever may be said in this direction, the fact remains to be seen next Saturday against Cardiff, whether or not the Pontypridd first fifteen are to show themselves worthy of such a distinction.'

Benefit Match

A few days after the Caerphilly match, a benefit match was played for a local charity. What is interesting is that it appears to be the first time that Maritime and

Pontypridd players had played in the same fixture. The Glamorgan Free Press reported:

'A long awaited match between Liberals and Conservatives, which consisted mainly of Pontypridd and Maritime men, was played in the presence of a large concourse at the Taff Vale Grounds on Thursday, February 5th 1891. The preliminary operations had been admirably carried out by Messrs W Evans and Fred Edwards, who were actuated with the commendable desire of promoting and extending interest in local football, and at the same time aiding the funds of the Pontypridd Free Library. After expenses had been paid, a considerable surplus remained. The crowd that gathered must have been just under 500, amongst whom were a considerable number of women.'

Men Against Boys

On February 7th 1891, the plucky Pontypriddian team proceeded to Cardiff to play a fixture which had been for some time been looked upon as necessitating unique form on their part before they could prevent an unprecedented score being placed against them. They arrived at Cardiff with some hundred supporters and put up at the Angel Hotel. At about 3.30 the teams faced each other on the Cardiff Arms Park. There were some six hundred people present, and immediately a remarkable contrast was visible between the two teams. Pontypridd appearing as mere boys pitted against opponents of Goliath proportions.

Pontypridd were fully represented with the exception of the two halves. The first half saw the Cardiff backs almost mysteriously passing the ball from hand to hand which dazzled the visitors, who although putting up a good front, only invaded the home territory once, thanks to individual play by Noah Morgan, Ack Llewellin, Ivor Howells and Christmas Jones. Meanwhile, the Cardiff team scored continuously and led by five goals and two tries to nil at half-time.

In the latter half the visitors more than held their own, and time after time did they frustrate the efforts of the premier team to score. The passing was now superb on the part of the Cardiff threequarters, but on each occasion their men were floored and the Pontypridd men were frequently applauded for their defensive tactics. The two Cardiff international centres, C S Arthur and Young, endeavoured to get over the visitor line, but were prevented by the tackling powers of the Pontypridd backs. Eventually, however, D W Evans scored another home try. Play was then waged in a spirited manner and for once Cardiff were compelled to play on the defensive. The Pontypridd forwards, for whom Ivor Howells, Ack Llewellin and Bill Williams were conspicuous, did great service and a good rush was only just stopped by Cardiff. Towards the end, Pontypridd came down with one of their notorious rushes, and George Harry, the wing, was only just prevented from scoring by Pearson intervening near the line. The final score ended in a resounding Cardiff win by five goals and four tries to nil (19-0).

The Pontypridd Chronicle commented:

'The "Red and White" lads attempted to fly at some high game, and to the delight of some bigoted persons, got a good sitting on. Still, there is some consolation for them in that they are not the only good team who have had a big let down on Cardiff Arms Park this season. If Pontypridd had played in the initial half with the same determination as they did after the interval, the score would not have been as tall as it was. Nevertheless, they have a return game, and if only they prepare, there is plenty of mettle in the team yet to "take it out" of even Cardiff. But this cannot be done without training, be they firsts, seconds or thirds for that matter. For the next month it means one of two things. They must either train or have heavy scores put up against them by Llandaff, Neath and Cardiff, all of whom have to visit the Taff Vale Ground.'

Revenge

On February 14th 1891, the long awaited return game against Llandaff took place, when the home team were looking for revenge for the heavy defeat in the initial game in Cardiff after losing three men through injuries. The homesters, though lighter than the visitors, beat them at all points of the game, which was well contested throughout. At lemon time, nothing had been scored by either side but had it not been for the selfishness of a home centre, who did not once give his wing man a chance, Pontypridd would have been winning by at least two tries. As it was, they scored three tries in the second half (3-0), the best by wing, George Harry. The Pontypridd Herald reported the game thus:

'At last - aye - at last, the defeat that so rankled in the bosoms of so many supporters of the "Red and Whites", has now been avenged, and for the present at least, breath freely. Speculation was rife as to the possible result of the struggle, some thinking it a matter of impossibility for Pontypridd to over-ride the score Llandaff had piled up in the first match, and others, taking into consideration the circumstances under which the score was made, favoured the chances of the home men.

The threequarter "par excellence" was George Harry, whose try was a scorching hot one. Fielding the ball within ten yards of his own line, he dodged for an opening and then literally flew over the rubicon, with Radley, the Llandaff sprinter, after him - aye - and even if the race continued to this day, its "after him" he'd still be, for the further they went, the further behind went the city man. The Pontypridd flyer on the right wing is at present in fine form and judging by the pace lately exhibited by him, he is in my mind the fastest wing, not only locally but in the whole of Wales.'

Christmas The "Flea"

Pontypridd then secured two home wins the following week. In the first, midweek, they narrowly defeated Merthyr by two goals and a try to one try and a drop goal (7-4), and in the second, on Saturday, Cardiff Stars by two goals and a try to nil (7-0). George Harry, the Ponty right wing, appears to have played twice on the Saturday afternoon! The Pontypridd Herald seemed unaware that he had damaged his ankle and gave these colourful reports:

'The Merthyr game was an exciting one, especially after Fred Thomas had scored an early try which put the homesters on their mettle. For Pontypridd, Alby Nicholas took Alun Morgan's place at fullback, and although he played fairly well, he wasn't to be compared to the youngster we are normally accustomed to see defend the sticks. Of the threequarters it would be hard to choose and it was pleasing to notice that they are taking to the passing game, a feature hitherto they had been markedly deficient in, still, there was great room for improvement! Ben Lewis and Noah Morgan were two "warm uns" in the centre, the former being most conspicuous on the aggressive, and the latter on the defensive. George Harry on the right wing had not much to do, but more than once he showed the Merthyrites a clean pair of heels. Gus Rowlands on the other wing, did exceedingly well, but received a nasty blow at the start, but this, however, did not prevent him crossing the rubicon on two occasions. Christmas Jones at half, played a clinking game, being as lively as a flea. If you have had the difficulty generally experienced in catching that ferocious animal, you will know what I mean, if not, the best way to describe it is: you put your finger on it and it is gone!

George Harry seemed a bit off colour against Cardiff Stars but perhaps this was the result of playing in two matches, having played for the 'A' team against Taff Vale Wanderers earlier in the afternoon, which would of necessity tell on any man. But wherever the blame lay,

George did not appear to be going at his usual pace. Another fault was that he was much too fond of recklessly throwing the ball away when near his own line. He should be cautioned about this, as if he persists in it, it will surely cost his team a match or two sooner or later.

Last week was a week of football with a vengeance, four matches in one week must break a record. The executive of the Pontypridd club are evidently trying to make up for the loss which the recent frost brought about. How far they have succeeded will be gathered from the fact that last week they encountered Merthyr and Cardiff Stars, whilst the 'A' Team played Taff Vale Wanderers and the Thursday 'A' team met Dowlais.'

Pride Restored

On February 28th 1891, the only match of importance locally was the Pontypridd v Neath match. Everyone thought it a foregone conclusion that Neath would win, but the homesters were determined not to knuckle under without a desperate struggle, at any rate, they had fully made up their minds that this match was not going to be a repetition of the previous meeting at the Gnoll, when Pontypridd were badly beaten by six tries to one.

One Pontypridd enthusiast before the game, said that he had dreamt that Pontypridd had won by a drop goal to a try. This dreamer, who was a playing member, professed to have had a vision, and said that at halftime the score would be Pontypridd nil, Neath one try, and that at fulltime Pontypridd would be winners by one drop goal to one try. And at halftime his vision was true, and looked even better when Benny Lewis dropped a marvellous goal for Pontypridd. The homesters were now on top and the dreamer's vision appeared to become reality, but Noah Morgan, the home centre threequarter, was forced to leave the field through injury and winger George Harry, was "knocked up", and, alas, the dreamers vision was not completed, as Neath dropped a goal and secured a late try to give them a two try and one drop goal to one try (5-3) victory. The Western Mail made the following comments that highlighted an injury to Noah Morgan, that seemed insignificant at the time but eventually, in hindsight, would have tragic consequences for the Pontypridd player. It read:

> 'Is is a strange fact that in their matches with Neath, Pontypridd have had more men laid out than in any other fixtures. Why? It is not known, for Neath by no means play a rough game, but so lucky (or unlucky) have the Pontypriddians been, that no less than eight players have been laid up after the two matches played this season. For three parts of the match the game was evenly contested, the homesters if anything having the best of it. Then fortune smiled upon Neath. George Harry and Noah Morgan, two of the home threequarters, were knocked out, the latter having to leave the ground.'

A Stinking Game

The Thursday after the Neath game, Pontypridd emerged victors in a home game against South Wales University, in a match that was described as *"totally devoid of incident, the only thing which at all excited the* spectators was the selfishness of the home halves, on whom execrations of an old blue colour and sulphuric odour are heaped in abundance". "Spectator" in the Glamorgan Free Press had this advice for club officials:

'I have growled at the Pontypridd committee several times this season, but I have a few more left. Why don't they have a rope around the goal lines so as to keep the crowds off, instead of having them crowding onto the field of play as they did last Saturday? This will always occur until the ends of the field, especially the town end, are roped off.'

Ack Llewellin
Pontypridd Captain 1890-91, 91-92, 92-93

Ack Llewellin pictured (centre) is without doubt one of the legendary players and administrators of the Pontypridd Rugby Football Club. His influence on the club started in the late 1880s and finished around 1923. During this time it was he and his brother Edward, who reformed the Pontypridd town team for the 1890-91 season. He captained the reconstituted club during it's first three seasons and when his brother moved to the North of England in 1893, he also took the reins as club secretary. A captain that led by example he was a stirling forward and when he retired he became a well respected referee and took charge of some of the Barbarian matches. He became the Welsh referee's representative on the Welsh Union from 1896 until 1922. He was a touch judge on that famous day in 1905 when Wales defeated New Zealand, and refereed the England v

Ireland match in 1906. He was also on the Glamorgan County Club committee for over fourteen years and was also a Welsh representative on the International Board. Unfortunately, the end of his involvement with rugby was brought about by a scandal over missing money from the local council offices, which ended in a prison term that must have left him a broken man. However, the Pontypridd club owe this man a tremendous debt, for he carried the name of the club into the higher echelons of Welsh rugby.

Maritime Colliery 1890

Match Of The Season

March 7th 1891, saw the first appearance in Pontypridd of the famous "black and blue" boys, Cardiff, and the "match of the season" which this was of course regarded, and had been the absorbing topic of conversation of local enthusiasts for all the week before the game. That Cardiff would win was a fact admitted by even the most sanguine supporters of the home team, but the question was, by how much? Looking at the chances from a sporting point of view, it was odds of two to one on, on Cardiff crossing the home line five times. This was early in the week, but when the game drew near, the number of tries predicted dropped from five to three. This of course was very possible, and many thought probable but subsequent events saw the redoubtable wearers of the blue and black able to cross only twice, and the last try they got was one of the flukiest tries ever scored, and would certainly have not been got but for the poor play of one of the Pontypridd threequarters.

The kick-off was unusually late, 5.15, and so the game was reduced to twenty-five minutes each way. Neither Pontypridd nor Cardiff were fully represented. Cardiff had representatives in the Wales team versus Ireland at Llanelly that day, and the home team were without Noah Morgan, and the valuable services of J Appleby, whose place was taken by J C Evans the Penygraig sprinter and a couple of forwards. The visitors were also unfortunate in that several well know faces were absent up front, and the only quartet obtainable was four centre threequarters. Pluckily as the homesters played throughout, they were still unable to cross the Cardiff line. Still, although beaten by a goal and two tries to nil (5-0), they were certainly not disgraced, for they all exerted themselves to the utmost.

The halftime score was Cardiff one try, Pontypridd nil, a slighter difference this time than in the initial match in Cardiff, when the home side were five goals and two tries to nil to the good. This, stated a local newspaper, reminded spectators of the song Charlie Coburn (another music hall star of the period) had scored his latest and greatest hit "Oh! What an alteration". The score when the final whistle sounded, was in favour of Cardiff, but loud and long was the shout of rapturous applause when it was seen that Pontypridd had made such a gallant stand, and every supporter of the "Red and Whites" was highly gratified with the result. The Glamorgan Free Press reported:

'The home custodian, Alun Morgan, played a sound game and is to be complemented on the show he made and "Jeremiah Juniper!" can't he put his foot to the ball! Of the threequarters, Benny Lewis, who did not as anticipated play on the wing was ubiquitous, and has seldom been seen to better advantage. "JC", who was recruited from Penygraig at the last moment, played a splendid game. George Harry, who was supposed to be having a rest due to a sore ankle, was at the last moment called upon, Jimmy Jim not being able to turn out, but did not shine. In fact, some people blamed him for allowing the second Cardiff try to be scored. Certain it is , however, that instead of running back to pick up, he should have allowed Alun Morgan to return.

40

At half, it was extremely pleasing to see the new-old form in the person of Eddie Gould (an old Ponty Stalwart), who it is hoped has come to stay, his display being worthy of his best days. Once in particular, it was odds on a thousand to gooseberry that he would score, and if only he had been endowed with a little more wind, all the forces of pandemonium itself would not have stopped him. Christmas Jones played a stirling game, in fact, to sum up, he gave the opposition a warm time of it. Of the pack, which played so well, it would be invidious to particularise individual play, but the other packs they have to meet in the future this season, will, I think, find them "foremen worthy of their steel".'

The Big Day Out

The Cardiff match at Taff Vale Park, was witnessed by a member of the Glamorgan Free Press reporting staff, who had not attended a "football" match before and in the March 14th issue gave this unique insight into a big match in these early days in Treforest:

'For the capital ground on which the footballer's of Pontypridd do battle with outsiders, the local team have to thank County Councillor James Roberts, who is in thorough sympathy with all healthy athletes having a tendency to benefit the youth of the district. As an infrequent onlooker, I was led by the glamour that somehow invests a struggle between a young Pontypridd team and a more pretentious and maybe more formidable rival, and in which the very nature of the case excites sympathy for, in the sense, one's own kith and kin, to fall in with the crowds that on Saturday last

were wending their way along the tramroad to the Treforest Football Ground.

On arriving at the field an animated sight presented itself. A large assemblage was arranged as to represent the three sides of a rectangle, the space having a goal at each end. We were informed that the gathering was the largest ever present for a football match in Pontypridd. Besides the human fringe of which I have spoken, a considerable number of sightseers were accommodated with seats and feet protectors in the grandstand. The stand is as decided advantage, since it enables ladies to be present and provides an almost certain immunity from bronchitic affections to weak and delicate mortals who rather than stand on damp ground for an hour or so, would be constrained to stay away.

As player after player passed the stand on the way to the dressing cabin, he was more or less cheered in proportion to the record he held in football playing. The strains of the Treforest Brass Band at a distance, was followed by the band itself, which took up its position in front of the grandstand. Very soon afterwards, the athletes made for the field and took up their stations of play.

Some people deprecate football as a dangerous game involving fractured limbs and broken heads. From what I saw I am fain to believe that there is at any rate a possibility of danger, since one enthusiastic player was doing his best for Pontypridd with limping strides owing to an injury sustained at a contest a week or two ago. Some players do sustain severe shocks by collisions and rough mauling to release the ball, there can be no doubt, but it is not yet proven that the balance of injuries of the classes lying to the credit of football, is any greater or more serious than those due to cricket, golf or hockey. At any rate, the recuperative powers of devoted players seems to be amazing, since whatever injuries are received, they are for the most part ready for active service within a few days.

When play began, it was pretty evident that the Pontypridd boys were under weighted, the visiting team being much heavier and bigger. I could not help noting the scientific and artistic elements that entered into the game when what is technically known as "a scrum" took place, a manoeuvre which to me suggested a gigantic variegated spider torturing a fly with its claws, and the Cardiff men seemed to be aimed at releasing the ball from the maze of legs by which it was surrounded, so as to place it within reach of their own supporting players outside, who seized it, dashing away, only to be pursued by the enemy as though the game of nations depended upon it.

The Pontypridd lads played gamely, and I should say splendidly but the weight of mettle was unmistakably against them and there are, and can be, no two options, that as they were defeated, which was to be expected, they were certainly not disgraced. I am inclined to believe that the Cardiff team made up their minds for an easy victory, instead of which they left the ground at "time" with a respect for their antagonists which is always felt by a generous conqueror who had just fought a foe worthy of his steel.

Finally, one important fact I noted during the interval between the first and second halves of the game. The resting contestants restored their exhausted energies not by alcoholic stimulants strange to say, but by absorbing the juice of lemon slices, supplied by Mr Parry-Thomas, of the Sportsman Hotel. For a game where endurance, energy and activity are required, this fact is a note in favour of the Rechabites.'

A Good Suggestion

Meanwhile, there were still whispers about an amalgamation between the Pontypridd and Maritime teams. The following letter appeared in the Glamorgan Free Press on March 13th 1891:

Sir - Might I suggest that some local gentlemen interested in football should endeavour to affect an amalgamation of the Pontypridd (recognised) and Maritime football clubs, if not all round, as least on special occasions when there are big matches. It is a pity to see a split allowed to exist from year to year, when a splendid team could be formed by adopting the course I suggest.

I remain
'A lover of football.'

Exciting Game Overshadowed

Following a creditable two try to one defeat (2-1) in Aberavon on March 14th 1891, Llanelly were the popular visitors to the Taff Vale Grounds a week later.

However, this date would become one of the saddest in the history of the Pontypridd club.

The Pontypridd boys were simply not in it with the "Scarlet Runners" and were defeated by two tries to nil (2-0). The Llanellytes came down like a wolf on the fold and although several of their best men were absent, they completely upset the calculations of the Homesters and notwithstanding the "Hillmens" vigorous efforts at defence, notched a large score to their credit. In wheeling and passing the Llanellytes were far and away above their opponents, who frequently appeared to be dropping into the arms of that gentleman the ancients called "Morpheus". Lloyd, Lovering, Rees and Nicholas, put in the horses work for the visitors, whilst Alun Morgan, Gould, Ben Tiley, Christmas Jones and Noah Morgan, were the most energetic on the home team. Such were the match reports but it was not until the newspapers were published the following Monday that the full extent of a tragedy that had occurred that afternoon became apparent to South Wales football enthusiasts. The Western Mail of Monday, March 23rd 1891, printed this report:

The Sad Death of a Pontypridd Footballer

'Noah Morgan, 24 years old, one of the threequarters of the Pontypridd football team that played on their ground with Llanelly on Saturday afternoon, died at his lodgings in Rhydyfelin, a short distance from the town, at 7.30 on Sunday evening. It appears that shortly before time was called, Morgan looked somewhat damaged and he fell to the ground. A number of football *friends ran to the spot and carried him to a shed close by where the players generally change their costumes. He soon became unconscious and a doctor was immediately sent for and a member of the team went for a conveyance to take him home. From enquiries amongst the combatants, it seems the poor fellow had not been hurt on the field of battle, and there was not the least mark of violence to be seen on him. He was carried home on a stretcher to his lodgings. Dr Howard Davies, who attended him, stated that the deceased had apparently died from a compression of the brain, caused by a ruptured blood vessel. Morgan worked at the Aberdare Tinworks, Treforest and was well known in Pontypridd.'*

The Inquest

On Tuesday, March 24th 1891, Mr E B Reece, Coroner, held an enquiry at the Duffryn Arms, Treforest, into the circumstances attending the death of the deceased, Noah Morgan, who resided with his parents at Rhydyfelin. Mrs Morgan, the mother of the deceased, stated that he was brought home unconscious after the match on Saturday last. Three weeks before, after the match against Neath, he had returned home complaining of a pain in the head. He was unable to work on the following Monday but subsequently appeared to be thoroughly well. Councillor Roberts, Treforest, said that he had witnessed the match and had seen the deceased turn as if to avoid one of the Llanelly players and appeared to lose control of his limbs. He fell to the ground and was immediately picked up and carried to a shed, where he was attended by Dr Davies and was subsequently taken home. He (Mr Roberts) had seen the deceased fall in a somewhat similar fashion in the match against Neath but after being take off the field he appeared to have completely recovered himself. James Nicholas had asked Morgan if he felt all right and received the reply "no, there is not much the matter". That was all he said on the field, but he did speak in the shed afterwards. Dr Davies said that he had found the deceased in a state of unconsciousness and upon examining him arrived at the conclusion that he had suffered from compression of the brain, caused by the bursting of a small blood vessel. There were no external injuries of any consequence, his head being free of marks apart from a few slight scars.

The jury brought in a verdict to the affect that *"the deceased died from a compression of the brain, caused by a rupture to a blood vessel resulting from a fall."* Mr Edward Llewellin, Pontypridd Football Club secretary, expressed the deep regret of the team at the sad event. The game had been a pleasant one throughout and there were no exhibitions of rough play on either side. The funeral of Noah Morgan took place on the following Thursday, March 26th 1891.

A few weeks later, the Glamorgan Free Press reported that the secretary of the Pontypridd Football Club had received from the Travellers Insurance Company, with whom the club were insured, the sum of £185, in respect of the death of Noah Morgan, which sum had been handed over to the mother of the deceased. Pontypridd's next two matches, against Bridgend and Abergavenny, went unreported, the likely reason being that they were postponed as a mark of respect to Noah Morgan.

Famous English Visitors

Pontypridd reappeared for the visit of the famous Northampton club on March 30th 1891. The game had created an amount of interest unparalleled in the annals of local football and the result could not have failed to be gratifying to the supporters of the "Red and Whites". No one dreamt of Pontypridd winning, and the visitors themselves had been led to believe by Llanelly a few days earlier, that the homesters were an easy touch. It had been thought locally that the scarlet clad visitors would probably win by about two goals, or that they would cross the Pontypridd line at least twice. The result, however, a victory for Pontypridd by two goals and one try to nil (11-0), showed how futile it was to gauge the approximate result of a match on past performances.

The match was a magnificent one from start to finish, the visitors, however, had the pull in weight and therefore the advantage in the scrums, but once the ball got air, the home eight rushed them off their feet. Behind the scrums as well, however good the visitors were at "the English game", they were on this Monday evidently non-plussed by "Taffy".

For Pontypridd, Alun Morgan at fullback, was palpably off colour, and made several serious mistakes. The home quartet, which had undergone radical alteration, played grandly throughout. Ben Tiley went back to his old place at centre, while Benny Lewis, it was seen, was also moved to centre. His try was the outcome of a combined bit of play which saw the ball passed from hand to hand with the rapidity of lightning, and fairly electrified the spectators, who gave vent to loud and continuous applause when they saw Benny "waltz" in with cowhide. At half, Christmas Jones fairly excelled himself and gained golden applause from the crowd for the manner in which he sat on Foster, whose fame had preceded him, being greeted with "éclat". Of the forwards, who all played well, it was invidious to single out anyone for special attention, suffice to say that every man justified his selection.

Jealousy Raises Its Ugly Head

The brilliant result for Pontypridd over Northampton, was somewhat marred by an argument with the committee of the Maritime Colliery team, who objected to one of their men playing for Pontypridd that day. The Glamorgan Free Press gave this account:

'The Pontypridd committee had, since the lamentable death of Noah Morgan, been in a fix as to whom to pick for the Northampton match. To extricate themselves from this predicament, they had decided to wait upon the committee of the Maritime Football Club, but before attending a meeting of that august body, some of them, in order to feel their way, first of all thought it wise to ask the members of the Maritime team whose services were required, whether they would play or not. An answer to the affirmative being readily forthcoming, they then made bold address to one or two of the most prominent Maritime committee men, who lo and behold, to their astonishment, were told that the Maritime committee had passed a resolution forbidding any member of their club assisting the town club. This news

appears to be from an undoubtedly good authority, and begs the question: If this is not professionalism, what is? The Maritime committee had no more claims upon the man than that contained in the mere playing of the substitute, unless there is something behind the scenes, which in this case seems rather likely, or why this arbitrary interference and intrusion upon the ordinary right of members when they have no fixtures of their own? But this "dog in a manger" policy was not confined to the non-playing members of the Maritime committee.

It is understood that Dan Radley played for their team that morning, but happened afterwards to state to an ex-officio member that he had intended going to the Sportsman Hotel, the headquarters of the Pontypridd club, to see some friends who had promised to meet there. On hearing this, fear leapt into the heart of the ex-officio, lest Radley should, if seen there, be asked to play for Pontypridd. He, therefore, prompted by the same selfish spirit that influenced the committee, brought all his persuasive powers to bear upon Radley in order, if possible, to keep him away from the Pontypridd HQ. But despite this, Radley, being a man and true footballer, at once saw through such despicable and jealous motives and decidedly told his babbler that he intended going, and what's more, that if asked to play, he would do so, which he did.'

'Spectator' in the same newspaper commented:

'Now, with all due respect to the members of the Maritime club, amongst whom I have many friends, I

must plainly say that such a policy is mad and selfish to a degree hitherto unparalleled in my experience of football, and only tends to widen the breach which exists between the two clubs, and were it not that I am intimately acquainted with some of the Maritime committee, I should say without a moments hesitation that such goings on could not possibly be the doings of sane persons, but rather those of some deranged fanatics who imagine themselves at the topmost rung of the ladder of football fame, and would therefore not desire to help those who by sheer determination, force and energy, have won through in first class football but whom labour under some cruel misapprehension or perhaps delusion, think they are beneath them - 'Fie Maritime Fie.'

Relations between the two clubs must now have been severely strained, but for a few weeks things appeared calm, but under the surface resentment was simmering, and later in the year bad feelings would again be aired in public.

Bad Referees At Aberavon

The first Pontypridd club had never encountered Aberavon, but when the reconstituted club had travelled to play them in Port Talbot, they had found the same difficulties there that other clubs had encountered. As the end of the season approached, on March 28th 1891, it was Maritime's turn to go there. The Glamorgan Free Press of April 3rd afterwards made these comments:

'The Maritime team journeyed to Aberavon on Saturday to do battle with the sturdy exponents of the

Winter pastime of the Avon valley. They, however, like most teams that visit Aberavon, were beaten, but not on their own merits. Strange to say, but all our local teams always seem to find fault with the referee in Aberavon, and now the same complaint reaches me from the supporters of the Maritime team. When I first heard of the "one-sidedness" on the part of the referee, I was with the Pontypridd 'A' team. A prominent member of the team came up to me after the match, and after mumbling something inaudible for a time, broke out with something like this - "What the blinking heck, if it wasn't for the blinking referee, we would have won!" Of course, I passed over this little incident thinking that it arose from the fact that his team had been badly beaten, and that the "blinking" individual referred to wanted to gloss over the defeat. But since then, both our premier teams have visited Aberavon, and since they all suffered from the same complaint, there must of course be something in it. However, Maritime can console themselves with the thought that although defeated, they were not disgraced.'

The Annual Dinner

The Annual Dinner of the Pontypridd Football Club was held at the Sportsman Hotel, on Thursday, May 7th 1891, when a large number of members and friends sat down to a repast served up by the host and hostess, Mr and Mr D Parry-Thomas. The vains (food) provided were the best, and coupled with the attention given by the host and hostess in their endeavours to cater for those present, gave unequivocal satisfaction. The room was suitably decorated for the occasion, flowers and plants serving to make the tables look picturesque and bright.

Along the walls were hung such mottoes as "Success to our Club", "Pontypridd to the Fore" and "Welcome to our Guests". Arranged at conscious intervals were coloured cards with such encouraging phrases as "Good old Ponty!", "On the ball Cardiff" and other phrases frequently used during the progress of the game. At the cross table which was erected at the upper end of the room, Mr William Spickett, an old Pontypridd footballer and captain, sat as chairman. He was supported on either side by the following guests and visitors - Messrs Treatt, D W Evans, Cardiff Football Club; M W Rees, Captain Penygraig Football Club; Moses Jenkins, Hon Secretary, Penygraig Football Club; E S Richards, Groves, Jones, J W John and others. The company having dined, the business part of the evening was gone through.

After the toast of "The Queen" was duly honoured, Councillor James Roberts took the chair and proceeded to present Mr Edward Llewellin, secretary of the Pontypridd Football Club, with a gold watch valued at £28, subscribed to by the members of the club as a token of their respect and as a symbol of the esteem with which they appreciated his services as secretary throughout the season. Mr Roberts referred eulogistically to the services of Mr Llewellin. The manner in which he had done his work was creditable in the extreme and he had often seen Mr Llewellin in the early hours of the morning down on the Taff Vale Grounds inspecting the field and keeping an eye on the weather. If any gentlemen undertook similar duties for the club, he hoped that they would fulfil them in the same manner in which Edward Llewellin had (cheers).

Mr Llewellin in reply, thanked them for the lovely present that they presented him. What he had done was only what anyone else undertaking similar duties would have done. He would promise them that if well backed up he would get the club still further advanced in the world of football. Pontypridd, in his opinion, had the makings of a club second to none in South Wales. Having thanked the members, Mr Llewellin, who was visibly affected, resumed his seat. Other speakers followed and bore excellent testimony to the services rendered by Mr Llewellin as secretary.

The next toast was that of "The Pontypridd Club", Messrs Ack Llewellin, Captain; J W Davies, Captain Thursday team; responded. Speaking of the matches with Cardiff, Ack Llewellin said that in the first match Pontypridd were defeated in a disastrous manner but the return match was proof of what Pontypridd could do. They were only defeated by the flukiest goal and a try, which he thought was creditable. The team altogether had done exceedingly well and he hoped that, under a better captain (No, No), they would do still greater things (Hear hear). He did not see any reason why they could not get up a club in Pontypridd as good as any in Wales (Cheers).

The Secretary's Speech

Mr Ted Llewellin, making the secretary's speech, said: "Our club, though known as a junior one, is one of the oldest in Wales, and some ten years ago could boast of a team that could make a good fight with anyone in the principality. I remember on one occasion we beat Cardiff on their own ground. At this time there were no other clubs in the district, and we had the whole of the Rhondda to select from. But the season after we beat Cardiff, we were to play Cwmbran in the cup, but only half our team turned up. As a result we were obliged to scrape up "Subs" from Cardiff, and even Cwmbran itself! Efforts were made year after year to organise a team but all to no avail. Although there were plenty of good players in the district, there was the drawback of men being unable to keep together. It was often the case that about Christmas time the interest in football waned, and most of the fixtures were cancelled. Matters went from bad to worse until the season before last, when everybody who had anything to do with the club gave the matter up in despair, thoroughly sick of the whole business. It was often galling for me to read reports of other clubs, knowing full well that Pontypridd, if only they put their shoulders to the wheel, could hold with the best of them.

Recent attempts to reorganise proved successful, and I am pleased to say that now the club is placed on a firmer footing than heretofore. After much trouble a good list of fixtures was arranged. Cardiff favoured us with a visit, as did Llanelly and Neath. Of the 31 matches played, 18 were won and 3 were drawn. The scoring during the year was 27 goals and 51 tries for, and 15 goals and 31 tries against, or 209 points to 119. This is not a bad show when it is considered that it is the result of practically a first season's display. No doubt much of this success is due to the way in which the committee worked, and to the splendid manner in which the players stuck together, but I think the greatest share of credit is due to our president, Councillor Roberts, without whose generous assistance we would never have been able to restart.

There is one thing that we may well be proud of, namely the good behaviour of not only our players, but also our spectators. Many of you are aware of the words of the Cardiff captain after their match here. He stated that he had bargained that in coming to Pontypridd that a rough and one sided game would be the result, but he had been agreeably surprised, as they were given a good pleasant game. The Neath secretary had also informed me that his men were very pleased with their visit to Pontypridd, and had written a letter to that effect. Llanelly and Merthyr had also spoken very highly of us. I hope our men will continue to give all teams that visit us a good reception, as it is the only way that we can get good teams to re-visit us. I have not experienced much difficulty in getting fixtures for next season, and I am sanguine that an even better list than last season will be forthcoming. It is a great pity that there will still be two teams in the town, but I think that we have done all that we can to get an amalgamation, but as the Maritime men are not disposed to fall in, we must do the best we can. If we persevere, we may therefore be able to do without their services. Certain it is that no first class clubs will play a club representing a colliery, managed by colliery officials, in preference to the town club.

Our financial position is not so bad considering the trying season we have just experienced. We spent between £60 and £70 on the ground, and we have been able to clear it off with the exception of £10. That is very satisfactory considering the exceptionally severe winter, the frost having deprived us of the proceeds of several good matches. I hope, if all turns out well, that we will be able to lay out another £50 on the field (cheers). I am sure, if the committee will work, and the players stick together as they did in the past season, and if our president will continue to take the same interest in us, that the success of next season will be secured.

The Final Toasts

A toast of "the Welsh Football Union" was proposed by Mr E S Richards, an old Swansea captain. In the course of an interesting speech Mr Richards said that it was only fair that the leading clubs should have prominence in the matter of selecting the international players over minor clubs, inasmuch as they had bigger membership enrolled, and had more representatives on the union committee. The toast was responded to by Mr Treat, Cardiff, and Mr A J Davies. Mr Edward Llewellin proposed the health of the club president, and Councillor Roberts in responding thanked the company for the manner in which the toast had been received, and promised to do as much in the future as he had done in the past. Mr Fred Edwards proposed the toast of "The visitors and kindred clubs". The rest of the evening was spent in a convivial manner, songs being rendered by Messrs Ivor Davies and others.

Maritime Committee Respond

The remarks by Edward Llewellin at the Pontypridd Football Club annual dinner about the club's failure to achieve an amalgamation with the Maritime Colliery team, brought a swift response from the Maritime

Secretary, which instigated a series of letters in The Glamorgan Free Press for several weeks afterwards, and gives us an insight into some of the things that had been going on that season. The "Free Press" of May 22nd 1891, carried this letter:

'Sir - Seeing a report of the Pontypridd football club dinner, I would thank you if you would give me a small space to reply to some of the statements made by their secretary with reference to our club.

In the first place, he says that his club has done all they ought to do, and it is not their fault that an amalgamation has not taken place before now. I should like to ask him, what has the Pontypridd club done towards an amalgamation? We, the officers of the Maritime Football Club know nothing whatsoever that they have done, unless trying to urge our players to play for their club can be called "doing all that they ought to". Also, he says that he does not think any secretary of first class teams would arrange fixtures with a team controlled by colliery officials, when there is a team belonging to the town. I suppose he was speaking to the three secretaries that were present. However, I fail to see myself where his remarks come in, re: "colliery officials controlling a club". Someone must control and manage it, and are not colliery officials as much entitled to, if they think fit to do so? I suppose that if the colliery officials to whom he refers to were assisting to control the Pontypridd club, it would all be well and good. But because they are not, I suppose that is why it is a sin in the eyes of the Pontypridd secretary. I am sure our committee has never received any assistance in getting our team together from anyone belonging to the Pontypridd club, and in fact, there was not a town team when we really formed our club.

We are wishful, and ever have been, to be on friendly terms with the town team, and only at the last Welsh Union meeting held in Cardiff less than a month ago, I met the Pontypridd secretary and suggested to him that we ought to arrange fixtures, pointing out to him the small expenses which would be entailed in playing two matches and the good gate which both teams would receive if we played, but "No!" was the answer "our committee are against you and think there ought to be only one team in Pontypridd".

There seems to be an animus against our club by the town team. We never heard of anything when there was a team at Treforest and another at Pontypridd (Maritime) about any ill feelings between the two teams, but now, since Treforest and Pontypridd have amalgamated they seem to think that everyone in the football world in this district ought to submit to them. We think, if there was room for two teams in the district before - one at Treforest and one at Pontypridd - there is room for two now, so we shall continue to go on as long as we receive the same support, which we undoubtedly do now. Thanking you in anticipation, Yours Truly,

Mr S Humphreys
Hon Secretary, Maritime Football Club

Edward Llewellin Hits Back

Edward Llewellin, not to be outdone, wrote this reply in the Glamorgan Free Press on May 29th 1891:

'Referring to the letter from Mr Humphreys, I should be glad if you would allow me a short space to make a few remarks thereon. Mr Humphreys, in the first place states that the officials of his club are not aware of any steps that have been taken towards an amalgamation of the existing clubs. If he only refers to the minute book of his committee, I think that he will find that some twelve months ago, they, at our request, considered the subject, and passed a resolution adverse to amalgamation.

With regard to my statement, that first class teams would not arrange fixtures with a team representing a colliery in preference to a representative town team, I think that the Maritime committee will find that my view is a correct one, and, although Mr Humphreys infers that he has arranged fixtures with Cardiff, Cardiff Harlequins and Penygraig for next season, I will leave it to your readers to see when their list of fixtures is published whether this is the case. Certain it is that upon present they have not arranged dates with at least two of the named teams.

It is untrue that when the Maritime club was formed that there was no town team, for with the exception of the 1889-90 season, the club has been in existence for the last fifteen years and only a week or two before their club was formed, several of their players were practising with our men on the Trallwng field. One of their players, Fryer, was not only a member of our club, but also of our committee, but he left us for Maritime, stating that he was afraid that unless he did so he would lose his job at the colliery.

I challenge Mr Humphreys to prove that either I or any member of our committee have subjected his club to any annoyance, or that we have endeavoured to induce any of their players to join our club. But on the other hand, instances can be given where supporters of his team have made efforts to entice players not only from our club, but from other clubs, with offers of jobs where they need not work much, yet earn a lot, so long as they are footballers. As to their being wishful to be on friendly terms with our club, I can only say that the manner in which they acted towards us with reference to our match with Northampton, did not show much feeling of friendship, but rather the reverse. I again repeat that I consider that there should be only one good club in Pontypridd, as through unity alone is there strength, but his view is not only shared by my committee but also to my knowledge by several of the leading players in the Maritime team, but for reasons well know to many of us, it would not do for them to join the town club. In conclusion, I deny that the position that we have attained in the football world since our happy amalgamation with the Treforest club, has made us dictatorial over local clubs, but to the contrary, we are getting along far better than the most sanguine of us had dared to hope, and it may be news to Mr Humphreys to know that I think, with one exception, we shall be able to arrange fixtures with ALL the first class teams in South Wales for next season, *whilst he on the other hand is, to use the words of the Cardiff secretary, "Writing begging letters for a fixture with our 'A' team".*

I am yours

Edward Llewellin
Hon Sec, Pontypridd Football Club
May 26th 1891

Another Letter From Maritime

As the weeks passed, the columns of the local newspapers continued to be filled with the arguments between the two club secretaries. The following letter appeared on June 5th 1891:

'Sir - I would thank you if you spared me a small space in your next issue to answer some of Mr Llewellin's statements in answer to my letter to you on the football organisations of Pontypridd. My object in writing that letter was to ascertain if Mr Llewellin (when he made his remarks at their dinner that he did not think that any secretary would give us fixtures, etc) was endeavouring to prevent our club arranging fixtures next season, when he made use of the words that I have quoted. I think that I am justified in assuming that this was his intention and every fair minded person who read your newspaper last week will think the same. We will, however, wait until our fixture list is published and let that prove what his interference has amounted to in regard to our club obtaining fixtures.

In his letter, he asks me to look at our minute book of about twelve months go or so, referring to a proposition of amalgamating. I adhere to what I wrote in my previous letter - that the town club has done nothing towards an amalgamation as far as we are aware. He admits that there was no town club during the season 1889-90, and as to the position to which he refers was passed during the 1889-90 season, it is impossible that the town club had anything to do with it. He also says that he knows nothing of their committee or himself trying to induce any of our players to play for Pontypridd, or of any annoyance which our club has been subjected to, and challenges me to produce evidence to that effect. Well, as an ounce of fact is worth any amount of argument, I beg to give an exact copy of a postcard of his, which I have in my possession, which one of our players received from Mr Llewellin:

Pontypridd Football Club
17 Wood Road
Pontypridd

Dear Sir - I am informed that you will play for us this season. If this is so I should be glad to see you come down to practice on Thursday evening at 6.30. Let me know if you will do so. We will pay all expenses and loss of time.

Yours Faithfully, Edward Llewellin

This is my answer to Mr Llewellin's challenge, which I give without further comment. In reference to his statement that our players have good wages and easy work promised, I leave this part of the letter to be answered by those who are better able to deal with it than I am. However, I must say in passing that it is nothing but pure invention so far as anyone who has authority in such matters either belonging to the club or colliery are concerned.

In regards to his remarks of wishing to be on friendly terms with us, he says the "Northampton affair" did not show much friendship, but rather the reverse. If we had not seen "Football Notes" in a local newspaper, which we deemed not worthy of notice, we should not have known what he meant by his reference to the "Northampton affair". I can only say this, that if the two gentlemen who represented them as a deputation from the town club, who came to ask on the Thursday night before Easter for some of our players to play against Northampton, had attended our committee meeting on the Friday night as they were invited and requested to do so, such committee meeting being specially convened to hear the application of the gentlemen, I have no doubt their request would have been granted, but as they never put in an appearance their request was never put before our committee.

In reference to what Mr Llewellin says are the words of the Cardiff secretary: "Writing begging letters for fixtures with their 'A' team" I make him a present of that statement. As a matter of fact, I have written but one letter and one postcard to the Cardiff secretary asking for fixtures, as I partly arranged with Mr Trent at the recent Welsh Union meeting, and I may say that I was courteously dealt with by him as any other secretary that we have arranged fixtures with has. With regard to the fixtures that the Pontypridd secretary says he has arranged, I am very pleased that so many first class teams will be coming to the district, and I am well aware that it is a benefit all round to get good teams to come to the town. At the same time though, we have fixtures gained by merit, and duly qualify for before we can secure them, which is not the case with the Pontypridd team, especially remembering the Cardiff fiasco, and other matches last season.'

Yours Truly
S Humphreys
Hon Secretary, Maritime Football Club

Postcard Explained

Back came Edward Llewellin with this letter in the Free Press of June 26th 1891:

'Sir - With reference to amalgamation. Will Mr Humphreys please state at whose request his committee considered the subject when they passed the resolution adverse to amalgamation? As to the postcard referred to, the following explanation will, I think, show that we acted squarely on the matter. Mr Murray, who then lived at Wattstown, had on one or two occasions during last Summer stated to members of our club that he was pleased to see that the town club had reformed, and that he had severed his connections with the Maritime club and would like to play for us. To make sure whether he really wished to join us or not, two members of our club waited upon him. He again informed them that he was anxious to play for us, and that he did not intend to again play for the Maritime team, and would not have done so the previous season had there been a town club.

I then sent him a postcard asking him to turn up to practice, and in due course received a reply written by Mr Harry Stead, the then secretary of the Maritime team, that Murray had promised to play for them, and as we anticipated, Murray shortly afterwards began work (?) at the Maritime colliery. Neither he nor any of the other members of the Maritime club were afterwards asked to play for us on any occasion when the Maritime had a match, but on the contrary, Murray time after time refused to play for us in certain of our matches even when his team had no fixtures. Their captain offered to assist us against Neath, whilst for our match against Cardiff two of the principal Maritime players volunteered their services. One of them, Connelly, would no doubt have been an acquisition to our team, but as the Maritime had a fixture that day I told him that we could not think of playing him.

On the other hand, the Maritime supporters have done all in their power to entice several of our leading players to play for them, and when those, who according to Mr Humphreys are in a better position to deal with this statement think fit to contradict it, I will then give instances.

Again, when our committee have thought it their duty to suspend any of our players, the supporters of the Maritime club have rushed with open arms to welcome them into their ranks, and though in one or two instances they had succeeded, I am pleased to say that our men were not long in returning to the fold, asserting that they would rather play for our 'A' team than for Maritime. Mr Humphreys states that our request for assistance *against Northampton was never put before his committee. If this is so, how and when was the resolution passed refusing to allow any of their players to assist us on Easter Monday? With reference to Mr Humphreys's closing remarks, in which he infers that the Maritime team gain their fixtures through "merit", then I will give them that credit, and as for our "fiasco" at Cardiff, I think it was a little more creditable than the Maritime display at Penygraig, when the would-be cupholders suffered defeat by the tune of three goals and five tries to nil.*

Yours Truly
Edward Llewellin
Hon Sec, Pontypridd Football Club
June 17th 1891

A Final Letter From Maritime

On July 3rd 1891, the Maritime secretary finally gave up the argument with the last letter in the Free Press:

'Sir - Will you kindly allow me again a small space in your next issue to finish the correspondence so far as we are concerned, which has taken place between Mr Llewellin and myself. I am now willing to leave the public to judge whether I was justified in writing to you my first letter, and nothing can be gained by further letters as Mr Llewellin has something new and equally groundless each time he writes, and, no doubt would have, if we kept on writing for all time.

Therefore, I decline to follow him in his last letter except for his charges about rough play. That charge did pretty good service last year, but I think it will not do for this. If the charge had come from some team whom we had played, and had later declined to arrange fixtures on those grounds, it would have been a little more appropriate than coming from him, and I think that the best answer to that charge will be when our fixture list for next season is published, and it will be found that we have arranged fixtures with one or two teams who that charge prevented us arranging games with last season, but have been able to gauge since then at their true worth such unfounded charges; and as I think nothing can be gained for the good of football by any further correspondence, I must decline to continue it any further. Thank you for granting me space in your several issues.

Yours Truly

Mr S Humphreys, Maritime Football Club, Pontypridd

Edward Llewellin's Last Letter

Edward Llewellin, never a man afraid of having the last word, had this last letter published on July 10th 1891:

'Sir - I was somewhat surprised to see Mr Humphreys's letter, which appeared in your last issue, that he so soon showed the "white feather", as I certainly thought from his previous letters that he would be able to furnish you with least half a column of misstatements for some time to come. He now leaves it to the public to judge whether he was justified in writing his first letter, and states that nothing can be gained from further letters, as I have something "new and groundless" each time I write. In Mr Humphreys's first letter he asserted that there was not a town team when

their club was formed; that we had done nothing towards amalgamation; that we endeavoured to induce their players to join our club, and finally, that they wished to be on friendly terms.

In my reply I showed that the town club WAS in existence when the Maritime club was formed; that at our request the Maritime club HAD considered the subject of amalgamation, but had passed a resolution adverse thereto; that we had not endeavoured to induce any of their players to join our club, but on the contrary, that supporters of his club had attempted to seduce players not only from our own, but other clubs as well, by offers of "Jobs where they do not need to work much, yet earn much"; that we had not subjected his club to any arrogance, and gave an instance of the manner in which the Maritimers in the past have shown "Friendship" (?) towards us.

In Mr Humphreys's second letter he carefully avoided, and I therefore take it for granted that he admits that our club was in existence when his team was formed; he did not deny that his committee had passed a resolution adverse to amalgamation, but inferred that the subject was not considered at OUR request; he attempted to show that we had endeavoured to get one of their players to join our ranks but left it for "someone else" to deal with the statement as to "offers of work and good wages" but so far "someone" has not thought it fit to contradict it; he stated that our request for assistance to play against Northampton had not been put before his committee, and wound up with the statement that his club had gained its fixtures on merit, and that we did not.

In my reply I required of Mr Humphreys, at whose request his committee considered the subject of amalgamation? I gave, I think, a satisfactory explanation as to the instance he quoted of our having endeavoured to induce one of their players to join our club, and gave instances of our having refused to play members of his club in our matches when they had fixtures. I enquired how and when his committee had passed the "resolution" refusing to allow any of their players to assist us against Northampton, and informed Mr Humphreys that if rough and brutal play were considered "merit" then we would give them credit. Mr Humphreys in his last letter refuses, and I am sure your readers will think with me, cannot answer the question plainly put to him as to amalgamation etc, but denies the charge of brutal play, and infers that we are not in a position to make that statement having not played them. I may say that the majority of our players have either played against or witnessed matches with the Maritime team, and that I am in a position to make that statement, and if Mr Humphreys will only favour the public with a list of "accidents" sustained by the opponents of the Maritime team during the season, I think it will prove what I assert.

I fail to see how Mr Humphreys can assert that he was justified in writing his first letter, or that I have something new and groundless to say each time I write, for I think that I have merely wrote in reply of his misstatements, not, however, that I cannot find something "New", for if only Mr Humphreys will continue with his correspondence he may well find that I know more then he is aware as to the workings of his club, and that we have nothing to lose by further correspondence, as OUR club is supported by true lovers of the game, with subscriptions from "friends", whilst his on the other hand, rides chiefly on the back of a public company, assisted by subscriptions collected in some instances by misrepresentations of the facts.

There is, however, one rather "old" matter to which I should like to call Mr Humphreys's attention. Some fifteen months ago, and previous to selecting a team to represent the district against Penygraig, it was arranged to play a scratch match on the Maritime grounds, and it was agreed that money received at the gate should go towards payment of the expenses of the team to Penygraig. Although our club paid those expenses, we have not yet received a penny from the Maritime club, but as we have written the account off our books as "Bad", I should be glad if Mr Humphreys would kindly send a cheque for the amount to the treasurer of the Free Library.'

I Am, Yours Truly
Edward Llewellin
Hon Secretary, Pontypridd Football Club

This letter seems to be the end of the debate but with such petty jealousies and arguments going on, it is hard to believe that twelve months later the two clubs WOULD amalgamate and Edward Llewellin and Mr Humphreys would work alongside each other on the same committee, but unsurprisingly, this did not last long!

71

Pontypridd RFC - Results Season 1890-91

1890

				For		Against	
				T	G	T	G
Sept 20th	Llanelly	Away	Lost	0	0	3	0
Sept 27th	Splott Rovers	Home	Won	3	0	1	0
Oct 4th	Pontymister	Away	Draw	0	1*	0	1*
Oct 11th	St Davids (Cardiff)	Home	Lost	1	0	2	0
Oct 18th	Cardiff Stars	Home	Won	1	0	0	0
Oct 25th	Neath	Away	Lost	6	0	1	0
Nov 1st	Caerphilly	Away	Won	1	0	0	0
Nov 8th	Penygraig	Home	Draw	0	1	0	1
Nov 15th	Aberavon	Home	Won	2	1	0	0
Nov 22nd	Llandaff	Away	Lost	4	1	0	0
Nov 29th	Pontymister	Home	Postponed				
Dec 6th	Merthyr	Away	Won	2	4	1	0
Dec 11th	Mountain Ash	Away	Lost	1	1	0	2(1*)
Dec 13th	Newport Harriers	Home	Postponed				
Dec 20th	Penarth	Away	Postponed				
Dec 25th	Cardiff District	Home	Postponed				
Dec 26th	Ely Rovers	Home	Postponed				
Dec 27th	Abergavenny	Home	Postponed				

* = Drop Goal
G + Goal (Converted try)
T = Try

1891

				For		Against	
Jan 10th	Penarth	Home	Postponed				
Jan 17th	Bridgend	Away	Postponed				
Jan 24th	Penygraig	Away	Abandoned				
Jan 31st	Caerphilly	Home	Won	2	3	0	0
Feb 7th	Cardiff	Away	Lost	0	0	5	4
Feb 14th	Llandaff	Home	Won	3	0	0	0
Feb 21st	Merthyr	Home	Won	1	2	1	1*
Feb 26th	Cardiff Stars	Home	Won	1	2	0	0
Feb 28th	Neath	Home	Lost	0	0	2	1*
Mar 3rd	S W University	Home	Won	?	?	?	?
Mar 7th	Cardiff	Home	Lost	0	0	1	1
Mar 14th	Aberavon	Away	Lost	1	0	2	0
Mar 21st	Llanelly	Home	Lost	0	0	2	0
Mar 30th	Northampton	Home	Won	1	2	0	0
Apr 3rd	Newport Harriers	Home	Won	2	3	0	0
Apr 11th	Cardiff District	Home	Won	2	2	1	0

Headquarters, Sportsman Hotel; Ground, Taff Vale Park; Captain First XV, Ack Llewellin; Vice Captain, Francis Miles; Second XV Captain, Reuben Richards; Vice Captain, Tom Evans; Thursday Team Captain, Walter J Davies; Vice Captain, Gwilym Morgan; President, James Roberts; Secretary, Edward Llewellin; Treasurer, Evan Williams.

The official club record read: P31 W18 D3 L10. FOR: 27 goals, 51 tries; AGAINST: 15 goals, 31 tries. Point scoring was introduced this season for the first time at international level by the international board, but was not introduced to club rugby for another two seasons. The points secured by using the international board guidelines would have been as follows: Try: 1pt; Conversion: 2pts (try and conversion recorded as a Goal); and a goal from a mark: 3pts.

Pontypridd RFC Second XV Fixtures
Season 1890-91

1890

Sept 27th	Dowlais	Away
Oct 4th	Pontymister 'A'	Home
Oct 11th	Pontyclown	Away
Oct 18th	Canton	Away
Oct 25th	Cogan	Home
Nov 1st	Cardiff Rangers	Home
Nov 8th	Penygraig 'A'	Away
Nov 15th	Aberavon 'A'	Away
Nov 22nd	Porth	Home
Nov 29th	Pontymister 'A'	Away
Dec 6th	Cardiff Cyclists	Home
Dec 13th	Cogan	Away
Dec 13th	Cogan	Away
Dec 20th	Penarth 'A'	Home
Dec 25th	Hafod	Home
Dec 27th	Taff Vale Wand	Away

1891

Jan 3rd	Dowlais	Home
Jan 10th	Penarth 'A'	Away
Jan 17th	Pontyclown	Home
Jan 24th	Penygraig 'A'	Home
Jan 31st	Cardiff Rangers	Away
Feb 7th	Penygraig 'A'	Home
Feb 14th	Porth	Away
Feb 21st	Taff Vale Wand	Home
Feb 28th	Hafod	Away
Mar 7th	Cardiff Cyclists	Away
Mar 14th	Aberavon 'A'	Home
Mar 27th	Penygraig 'A'	Away
Mar 28th	Canton	Home

CHAPTER TWO

THE SECOND SEASON -
MARITIME GROW IN STATURE
AMALGAMATION RUMOURS
THE FINAL AGREEMENT

The second season of the reconstituted Pontypridd Football Club would see it reach several highs and lows. They would also suffer again through injuries, which saw some players retire from playing altogether. The two matches against Cardiff Harlequins in particular were very rough, and during the first encounter, centre threequarter, Jack Dyke, received a serious injury and his replacement for the next game, Gus Rowlands, brought in from the Treforest Wanderers club, also received so severe an injury that he was laid off work for several weeks and was never seen wearing the 'Rhone' again. After being knocked out in one game, Ponty half, Christmas Jones, acted as a touch judge against Neath, and was said to have gained more ground in that position than when he was playing! Walter Davies was unfairly treated, appearing on the wing early in the season, he was moved by the match committee to the forwards and was promptly dropped for not doing well there!

Ack Llewellin was reappointed captain for a second time, and with Bill Williams and Ivor Howells, were the backbone of the Pontypridd pack. A newcomer, Matt Nicholls, looked a good prospect early on, but later remarks such as: "He must stop playing to the crowd, and get into the middle of the squash where he should use his immense strength to advantage" became a common comment. The eight, as a whole, were considered rather small and were continually beaten in the set pieces but their agility and speed made them formidable when the ball was in the loose. At half, the club had problems, several players being tried; Bridge Merry and Christmas Jones being one combination tried, but were considered a rather weak pair, and Hill, from Abergavenny, was for a time brought in to try and strengthen the positions. The centre position, throughout the season, was plagued by injuries, with veteran Mountain Ash man, Ben Tiley, being the outstanding but erratic favourite early on, while on the wings Alf Lewis and his brother Ben, played well, while the latter was also tried at half and also at fullback when Alun Morgan was tried at centre. The first choice at fullback was Alun Morgan, who despite being a bit of a character, was an outstanding player, and was amongst the first on the team sheet every week.

The outstanding result of the season was the home victory over Cardiff, but throughout the season the major topic of conversation was still the rumoured amalgamation with the Maritime Colliery team. The latter club would partially open the door when they cancelled a lucrative home game against the Welsh Wanderers so that it would not affect the gate in aid of the injured Pontypridd centre, Gus Rowlands. The Maritime club itself would have a more successful season than Pontypridd, even with an improved fixture list and secured an impressive draw at Llanelly. One of their forwards, Jimmy Connelly, appeared in the Welsh international trials. In January 1892, "bard" in the

Pontypridd Chronicle wrote: *'I think Connelly stands a good chance of getting his headgear in the Scottish match, and the contest should be between him and Jim Boucher, who was the only man who could keep him out. Boucher is one of the fastest forwards in Wales, so it would be all the more honour for Jim and local football if he did get in.'* However, it was not to be and Connelly did not earn his international cap.

The 1891 Annual General Meeting

The annual general meeting of the Pontypridd Football Club was held at the Sportsman Hotel on July 23rd 1891, where a large number of local enthusiasts and nearly all the old members were present. The meeting was presided over by Mr Teddy Lewis. The secretary, Mr Edward Llewellin, submitted last season's balance sheet from which it appeared the receipts amounted to nearly £200, and after spending about £60 on improving the Taff Vale Grounds, there was a balance of about £5.

The election of officers then took place. Councillor James Roberts was unanimously re-elected as president of the club. Ack Llewellin was re-elected first XV captain, with Francis Miles as vice captain. Mr R F Davies (Coffee Tavern), was elected captain of the second team, with Mr D Evans (Treforest), his vice captain. A large general committee numbering about thirty was also appointed with the power to form a match committee. It was mentioned that subscriptions should remain as before, and that season tickets would be limited. After the business part of the evening the members passed the rest of the evening in an enjoyable manner.

The New Season's Team

The Glamorgan Free Press previewed the season like this:

'This year the first team should be stronger than ever. Ben Tiley, will once more be donning his shirt and if his leg keeps alright he should be a useful acquisition for the team. Mr Ack Llewellin has again been selected as captain, and most thought that a better man could not have been chosen. He is a good player and has a great deal of influence on the other players. The promising youngster, Alun Morgan, will again play custodian; Ben Tiley, Alf Lewis and Ben Lewis, will be the threequarters and tricky little Christmas Jones will be at halfback. The forwards will be pretty much as the previous year. This being the team's second season together, it is thought they should show some splendid combination. If this is so, it is hoped Pontypridd will have one of the best sides in South Wales, and, it is thought, with luck, that the international match committee might find it worth their while to notice some of the Pontypridd players.

There is a splendid grandstand on the ground and a pavilion for the players. Previous to the initial match of the season, the committee, captain and secretary, have been actively engaged in improving the ground, and have completely railed the field from goalpost to goalpost. Besides this, extensive alterations have been made to the grandstand to ensure the comforts of the visitors, while the level of the field has been properly laid out. With an eye to business, arrangements have been made for enlarging the entrance to the grounds. What stood for an entrance before, has been replaced by a large gate suitable to pass a large body, including that of the amiable Mrs Brown, who cannot now have further complaint of the egress (exit). An ash footway has also been laid from the entrance to the grandstand, and every facility has been given to allow everyone to obtain a good view of the game. It is thought that by no means now can spectators interfere with the players.'

Several practice matches were played proceeding the season's start, and Christmas Jones showed excellent form and was as tricky as ever. Alun Morgan never failed to make his presence known, while Reuben Richards showed himself equal to a position in the first team. However, the team looked likely to consist of the players that did duty the previous season. Indications were that the second XV would come out in advance of any other second class team in the district, as many young players from other towns had moved into the district. On the whole, prospects for the season were most satisfactory for the Pontypridd representatives.

The Pontypridd Captain

Mr Ack Llewellin, who rendered such splendid service last season, will again captain Pontypridd this season, which promises to be one of the most successful on record. He is a Monmouthshire man, having been born in Abergavenny in December 1866. His height is six foot and weighs eleven stone eight pounds, and altogether is regarded as one of the finest athletes in the town. He is an ardent lover of the manly game of football and has been playing constantly for the last ten years. For years he was one of the most prominent members of the Abergavenny team, and when three years before this season, he came to Pontypridd, where he was at once secured a place in the Treforest XV, who at that time were the premier team in the district. When, subsequently, a representative town club was re-formed, Mr Ack Llewellin was unanimously selected as captain, a selection that had been more than justified. Mr Ack Llewellin holds a responsible position in a Pontypridd office and is most popular with his fellow townsmen.

Maritime Prospects

The Maritime Colliery team, although deprived of many of their prized players, are going to make a bid for premier honours. Although the rumoured amalgamation with the Pontypridd club was far from being secured, it was expected that good relations will exist throughout. Tom Murray, Harry Williams, Tom Hemsworth and Jack Hope are all in good condition and are likely to cause much trouble to opposing teams during the season. Steve Sullivan and Tudor Foster are absentees this season. The arrangements at the Maesycoed ground were everything that could be desired, and their fixture list bears comparison with any other club.

The Maritime Captain

Mr Benjamin Dickenson will be the Maritime captain this season. He is a fine young fellow of twenty-six, with a height of five foot nine inches, and turns the scales at twelve stone nine pounds. He hails from Castleford, Yorkshire, and came to Pontypridd in 1886 to undertake the duties of fireman at the Maritime Colliery, where hundreds of Yorkshire lads are employed. He had taken little interest in football in Yorkshire, and it was not until he joined the Maritime team in 1888 that he applied himself seriously to the game. He played centre-threequarter, and in 1889 was elected captain, and at the last general meeting the honour was once more unanimously conferred upon him.

The Season Begins

'From its kick off, throw it out, form a decent scrummage. Keep it loose, splendid rush, bravo, win or die.'

These were the sentiments expressed by the local propellers of the cowhide on the day that witnessed the inauguration of the 1891-92 season, when Newport Harriers were the visitors on September 19th 1891, and naturally looked forward to their initial match with eagerness, though there were those who were decidedly anxious lest the Pontypridd boys should under rate their opponents, and wind up their opening match with the balance on the wrong side. This, however, did not happen and although the Newportonians were in better form than the home lot, it could not be denied that the best team had won, and had Pontypridd's scrummaging been in better fettle, their score would have been much bigger than six points to two.

At forward, the visitors had a decided advantage, thus sternly and amply demonstrating to the homesters that preference should be given to those players who go in for training, for if the forwards alone could have won the match, there would have been only one team in it, and that was not Pontypridd! Of course, Pontypridd were missing Eddie Gould, but that is no excuse for the miserable condition in which most of the forwards appeared, whilst to make matters worse, the homesters played with five men at threequarter! The best of a poor lot of forwards were captain Ack Llewellin and Raymond Watkins, whose try was one of the best ever witnessed by a forward on the Taff Vale Grounds. At threequarter, Jack Dyke, the old Cheltonian, was far and away the best. His try was described as a 'red hot 'un' and the manner in which he put Alf Lewis over in the corner was a treat. Picking up in fine style directly under his own posts, he fairly electrified players and spectators alike by beating the Newportonians, and when outside his own 25, passed grandly to Alf Lewis who was waiting outside him, and the veteran sprinter, going like a racehorse, planted the oval behind the visitors posts. The Pontypridd team for the first match of the season was:

Fullback, Alun Morgan; Threequarters, Alf Lewis, Ben Lewis, Jack Dyke, Walter Davies; Halves, Jack Ewans and Christmas Jones; Forwards, Ack Llewellin (C), Bill Williams, Ivor Howells, Lancaster, O Bowers, Francis Miles, John James, Raymond Watkins.

Much Kindness From 'Ma'

When Pontypridd met Cardiff Stars at the Taff Vale Grounds on September 16th 1891 and the teams lined up at 5 o'clock, both teams were at full strength. The homesters won by seven points to four, but the Free Press reporter was none too happy and wrote:

'This match was nothing short of a farce, and the lovers of such are recommended to visit the grounds of the Pontypridd team when the first XV are playing, where they would be delighted by what they find there, more especially at forward. There was never any class about the football, and although the home team that turned out included several experienced men, they have much to learn about combination.

The best team lost, and that is certain, and again the home team had to thank their backs, for the pack were simply rotten. Not on one solitary occasion did they have a look in, and again it was said that the match committee should make it imperative that the forwards who so disgusted onlookers either train, or they put out an entirely new lot. The only men who showed anything like form, and even they were along way off what they ought to be, were Ray Watkins, Bill Williams and Lancaster.'

A week later, the Glamorgan Free Press gave this report of an injury and its aftermath, to Pontypridd player, Jack Dyke:

'I am sure everyone will sympathise with Mr Jack Dyke, who received so severe an injury during the match that he is only able to get about on crutches, and none are more sincerely sorry than I am. He should, however, have left the field immediately, but expressing contempt for his injury, he struggled on. In the Sportsman Hotel after the match, I must confess that I was agreeably

surprised at the attention bestowed upon the gentleman in question. The way in which the genial hostess was attending him, and the cheering manner in which she spoke, was not to be rivalled by the tenderest mother's care and methinks it must have soothed the sufferers pain to an extent almost uncreditable to those who have not had the pleasure of meeting the amiable Mrs Thomas. Small wonder indeed that Mr Dyke felt relieved after her careful treatment, who would not? It almost tempted me to do something to injure myself, but I was afraid that I should be conveyed home and thereby robbed of the tenderly and motherly nursing of 'Ma', as she is know to the team. Such kindness cannot be forgotten, and I venture to think that should Mr Dyke leave town tomorrow, he would carry the kindest recollections of the hospitality afforded him under the roof of the Sportsman Hotel.'

Woe, Consternation And Dismay

On October 3rd 1891, Pontypridd journeyed to do battle against the sturdy representatives of the 'Tinplate town', Llanelly, their meeting with whom had been the subject of much speculation in as much as the form shown so far by Pontypridd was not calculated to inspire their supporters with much confidence. Still, it was thought that they would exercise every power to avert a crushing defeat, but when the telegram conveying the result was received at the club headquarters, woe, consternation and utmost dismay was written visibly on the faces of those who had been left at home. However, there was nothing to do but shiver over the thought of the appallingly high score of four goals and one try to Llanelly, to one try to

Pontypridd (or 22-2), until the team return home, when it was thought maybe possible that by some means they might be able to remove the load that weighed on them so heavily.

At half past three o'clock, the teams stepped into the arena clad in the same coloured jerseys, the Llanelly men being distinguished by white pocket handkerchiefs, which encircled their arms, but as the game wore on, the badges loosened, and were strewn across the field. The match itself was grandly contested throughout, and though it would hardly be fair to say that Llanelly were not the better team, the visitors were handicapped by the absence of Jack Dyke and Ivor Howells, two of their best men, who were unfortunately unable to travel. Despite this heavy defeat, 'Toricus' in the Free Press, gave this advice:

'Should the clubs who figure on Pontypridd's fixture list presume that because they were beaten by a tall score, that they cannot play football, then a rude awakening is in store for them, for unless I am mistaken, they will secure a very respectable position by the end of the season.'

The Pontypridd team that day was:

Fullback, Alun Morgan; Threequarters, Ben Tiley, Ben Lewis, Alf Lewis, W J Davies; Halves, C Jones and J E Ewans; Forwards, Ack Llewellin (C), Francis Miles, J Nicholas, D Walters, J R Watkins, C Francis, J A James, W Williams.

A Tear Fell Gently

The following Saturday, Pontypridd went down to a two goals to nil (10-0) home defeat by Morriston. Local reporters gave their views of the game in colourful tones. 'Gladiator' in the Pontypridd Chronicle wrote:

'A tear fell gently from my eye when the final whistle sounded "no-side" and left Pontypridd the losers. Defeat by two goals to nil running so close upon the Llanelly defeat makes an uncomfortable feeling creep over me. These defeats are certainly not very encouraging. The new season has not opened very encouragingly for Pontypridd and I begin to fear the result of the Caerphilly match next Saturday. However, I will hope for the best. Yet after all, why should I write in such mournful tones, when after the game a well qualified gentlemen told me that "the best club lost the game taking into consideration that the superiority was on the side of the homesters". I can't say that I agree with this statement in total. The home boys did play a vigorous game I admit, but there were occasions - and frequent occasions I am sorry to say - when both the forwards and backs lost ground through irresolution. I have often noticed in cases where the visiting team puts in a vigorous attack early in the game, that the homesters seem, as the old phrase goes, "Completely taken back" and do not recover until the second half. Let the Homesters in future remember that it is quite important to score in the first half as in the second. Albeit, the 'Maron Lads' did not make such a bad show. Reviewing the incidents of the match in deliberation, I feel constrained to express the opinion that the defeat

was one of those unfortunate circumstances which cannot always be avoided. The two goals obtained by the visitors were not the result of any special skills, but were gained during the excitement of scrummaging on the verge of the home line.'

On the same day, the Pontypridd 'A' team were defeated by Canton 'A' by a try to nil. A local newspaper commented:

"The game itself was all in favour of the visitors, but as they had to play sixteen men, inclusive of the referee, the wonder is that they did so well."

Jack Stays Clean

On Monday, October 12th 1891, a home match against Caerphilly was carried out in adverse conditions, with rain rendering the Taff Vale Ground relative to a quagmire. The home team finally came out of their shell in something like form and administered a crushing defeat of one goal and five tries to nil (or 15-0), on the representatives of the ancient town of Caerphilly. Considering the slippery nature of the ground and ball, they were to be congratulated on achieving a victory as creditable as pronounced, and with only a moderately good team too! Gus Rowlands was tried amongst the quartet, and to say he was a success poorly describes the really good exhibition of the game played by the young and inexperienced player. When he had the honour of captaining the Treforest Wanderers, Gus was always foremost on a wet and muddy day, fielding the ball beautifully and tackled with a spirit and determination which soon made a name for himself. All these remarks can be applied to the way in which he played against Caerphilly and the field committee are recommended to once more try him in the first XV. Jack Ewans, substituting for Alun Morgan at fullback, was intensively amused at the rest of his team rolling around in the mud, while he himself remained untouched and unsoiled, with the exception of his boots.

Adverse To Good Breeding

A home match against Splott Rovers on October 24th 1891, was played before a large crowd, but turned out to be one of the dreariest matches ever witnessed on the Taff Vale Ground. The Pontypridd Chronicle was very critical of the visitors and wrote:

'It was evident from the start that the visitors were fairly outclassed, and had they played the game the score would have been much greater than two goals to nil (10-0). They had all the appearance of having been let out of jail for the day, but the pity was that there was no-one to take care of them or to be responsible for their actions. Taking into consideration their ungentlemanly conduct, many hope that Pontypridd will not give them another fixture. The home team were streets ahead of their opponents, who appeared to possess only a crude knowledge of the rules affecting the game. This lack of knowledge could, however, be easily pardoned, but the manner in which they expressed themselves was decidedly adverse to good breeding, and as evil practices corrupt manners, those present hoped it would be the last opportunity to see 'the spotted Rovers' on the Taff Vale ground.'

Taff Vale Park

Taff Vale Park, Pontypridd

On The Way To The Match!

The High Street, Graig, Pontypridd (photographed around 1888) was just one of the routes that could be taken to reach the Maritime Colliery team playing ground at Maesycoed. As the Glamorgan Free Press remarked, to take this route up the Rhiw Hill was *'as steep as climbing the Alps'*.

Meanwhile, the same day the Pontypridd 'A' team were having an unpleasant time in Porth. It was reported that it was a pity that the Porth team should gain discredit through the ungentlemanly and unsportsmanlike manner of just one of their players, who fairly disgraced not only himself but also his team. The Porth committee were urged to dispense with his services if they wished to uphold the honour of their club.

Fourteen Man Pontypridd Battle Hard

A good load of enthusiasts had accompanied the Pontypridd team to the Belle Vue Ground, Penygraig, on October 31st, and these had considerably swelled the already large gate. Those assembled were rewarded with a really grand exposition of the rugby code, Pontypridd and Penygraig being well matched, while the play throughout was fast and exciting. In the first half, the defences of both teams were so good that nothing whatsoever was scored, but Pontypridd experienced deuced bad luck in losing winger, Ben Lewis, less than five minutes after the start, a loss that put them in a very disadvantageous position. Scorning this loss, however, they played with the utmost vigour and instead of being continually beaten, as would have been supposed, they introduced fresh energy and gave the homesters a warm time of it. In the second half, the pace was simply terrific, every man playing for all he was worth and though not wishing to be uncharitable, the winners pulled the match out of the fire with the most veritable fluky try imaginable. The crowd, however, could not, or would not, see this, judging from the cheering, yelling, hat waving and stick shaking which ensued when Evans got over in the corner of the only score (2-0) of the match. Considering that Pontypridd only had fourteen men, much credit was due to them for the uphill fight, of which their followers had just cause to be proud. 'Marcus' in the Pontypridd Chronicle reported:

'This match was certainly rough. First of all Benny Lewis got seriously hurt, and will not be seen on the field again for a long time, then Christmas Jones obtained a punch to the anatomy from Rees's knee, whilst Jack Ewans tried to gain the sympathies of the crowd by rolling over and laying out supinely when someone ran against him, though it is but only fair to say that he took it in quite a sportsmanlike fashion. Then there was the charging, tripping, pushing and wrangling heterorganeously, and the referee had a lively time of it. Gammon and Evans, for Penygraig, infused into their play more of the "fortiter in re" than the "suaviter in modo" style and despite the powerful kicking and running of Rees and Stoddart, they were all tarred by the same brush.'

Absence Of Confidence

Pontypridd travelled to Penarth on November 7th 1891 and were soundly thrashed by fourteen points to nil. At times this season they had performed smartly, while at other times they had been just as streaky. In the previous match they appeared to have had a capital chance of beating Penygraig, but luck more than anything was against them. However, a most extraordinary change came over their play against Penarth, and they fell in the direst way possible, and from first to last were simply not in it. The "Seasiders" ladled out a gruelling in an unmistakable manner and fairly took Pontypridd's breath away. 'Marcus' in the Pontypridd Chronicle commented:

'I attribute such a heavy defeat to the absence of confidence which is the making of the team. Some teams have so little confidence away from home that they often get beaten by teams not worthy to stand on the same field and although Pontypridd sometimes suffer a similar fate, it was not the case this time.

But I heard a person remark this week that Ponty had made a 'splendid stand' against the seaside combination. RUBBISH! Whoever says so knows no more about football than the printers devil, and whose knowledge is confined to kicking a bundle of rags or paper about the streets, when sent on an errand. There was only one player there, in fairness, who made himself conspicuous by atoning in some measure for sundry mistakes by his comrades, I refer to the custodian, Alun Morgan, who repeatedly cleared his line and got the ball away when labouring under the disadvantage of a rather shaky quartet. He created a very favourable impression on the Penarth supporters, but the other threequarters, with the exception of Gus Rowlands, were not worth much. At half, Christmas Jones improved steadily, his tackling powers deserving special mention. Bridge Merry will strengthen the team when he gets used to the remainder of the backs. The committee are said to be considering changes in the front rank. There is great room for improvements I dare say, but they must take care that in taking a man out they do not put in a man who is inferior.'

Not Called a "Ground" Any More

The same day as the First XV went down at Penarth, the Pontypridd 'A' team defeated their Penarth counterparts at Treforest. However, the Pontypridd Herald reported an event that would change the name of the playing field forever:

'The 'A' team were victorious on the Taff Vale Grounds, beg your pardon, Honorary Secretary Ted Llewellin, I should have said 'PARK'. I had momentarily forgotten that you have taken your flight far, far above the degenerate terms of 'ground' and are no longer willing the home of the 'Rhone' lads will ever again be easily designated. However, 'ethuldgin sie mich es soll nicht nicht mer vorcomen.'

Guidance For Referees

For a home game against Pontypridd on November 14th 1891, the match committee had undertaken a complete alteration, the centres having been shunted and their places being taken by Mat Nicholas and Alun Morgan. The forwards were practically as before, except Synnick, of Gloucester City fame, who had been found a place in the pack. Pontypridd were confident in their ability to give the visitors a licking, but they failed to realise these sanguine expectations, and had to put up with another reversal. It was a fiery struggle, in which hard knocks and savage keenness prevailed. In the scrums the visitors were on top, but the home side ruled the loose and rarely failed to gain ground, and the wonder is that the 'Rhone' lads did not see this until well into the second half, after which they had the better of the play and succeeded in

94

scoring a try, which was disallowed for some reason by the gentleman (?) officiating as referee.

'Toricus' in the Glamorgan Free Press commented:

'There was joy down in Pontymister when the result came to hand, especially when the conquering heroes returned home victors by one goal and two tries to nil, though they owed just a little something to the referee who despite all his good intentions, did not by any means possess the necessary qualifications for one in such an onerous position. He complained that he had been badly treated, but he may well congratulate himself that he got off as he did. By the foregoing, I do not wish to convey the impression that I was one of those who wished to dip him under the 'sweet smelling' waters of the River Taff, but as a spectator I could not but help remember that while touring in 'broadacreshire', I saw a referee receive a 'very friendly greeting' with such harmless 'toys' such as pop bottles, pieces of turf, sticks, stones and last but not least, eggs, which if not rotten, must have come from a hen in a very critical state of health, and all this for less trespass of the rules than which occurred during this game on the part of the referee, who should read, mark, learn and inwardly digest the page in the rule book under the heading 'Rules for the Guidance of Referees'. The game itself was rough, the visitors being predominant in this characteristic, as they were also with the tongue, with which they could give most teams a start. Be this as it may, if we are to be favoured with any more such games, I shall not be present, as my language will not run to it!'

Maritime Mudlarks And A Cap For Jimmy?

On November 21st 1891, the Maritime Colliery team lost its unbeaten record for the season when they were defeated by a try to nil (3-0) at Llandaff. The following Saturday, Pontypridd's home fixture was postponed, but Maritime tried to play a home fixture with Penarth. 'Marcus' in the Pontypridd Chronicle wrote:

'There were some thirty strong candidates for the washtub at Maesycoed last Saturday, and soap and water must have been in great demand at the Rose and Crown afterwards. Poor spectators? I for one was nearly drowned, but what price the players? During the short half-hour which play occupied, those thirty young imps slipped, fell and danced about in the mud like a lot of lunatics. That's rather harsh, but if I had done the same thing I would pardon anyone applying a similar term. Harry Stead caught my eye while playing and nodded. I could hardly refrain from laughing at the mud which smeared his countenance. Under such circumstances it is hardly to be wondered that Penarth thought it advisable to discontinue the match after the interval.'

'Marcus' continued:

'Maritime forward, Jimmy Connelly is sparing no pains to get himself in form for the international trial at Cardiff on Monday. If what I hear is correct, a certain medical man (Dr Howard Davies - local medical officer for the Pontypridd Board of Health - Ed.) who takes an interest in the welfare of the Maritime club, is instructing Jim on his course of diet. In fact, he is training the young son of Erin for the event. If you succeed in gaining the

coveted honour, Jim, my lad, I'll drink your health in champagne!

Roughness In Cardiff

When Pontypridd were due to travel to play Cardiff Harlequins on December 5th 1891, the 'Rhone' supporters were not sanguine of the result of the match. 'Marcus' in the Pontypridd Chronicle, had these words before the game:

'There is certainly a lot of uncertainty about Pontypridd, but as for glory - not much. I'd lay odds that before the start is made, every players heart - or pluck, whatever words my readers care to apply - will be in the region of their boots. Every footballer knows that there is nothing more desirable in a team as combination but how can the Pontypridd committee expect their team to acquire such a desirable quality if from week to week there is all this shifting, chopping and changing of the team 'all over the shop'? I do not care about drawing comparisons, but I think if the other team in our midst, Maritime, had not played the same men continually, they would not now hold the high position that they now do. I do not care about perpetually trying to hammer into the heads of the committee some of my own ideas, but as my avowed intention is to endeavour to improve our Winter pastime, I consider it my duty to talk to them in a strain that they cannot fail to understand. There are some ugly rumours afloat, as to a general flare up amongst the committee and officers. I will not vouch for its accuracy, but I hope, if there is a little storm, that it will soon blow over.

The match itself at the conclusion, would long be remembered by the representatives of the town at the junction of the Rhondda, as one of the roughest in which they had ever participated. Gus Rowlands, who was undoubtedly one of the best threequarters in the principality, broke his collar bone and would not, it was feared, don the colours again, at any rate not this season. Christmas Jones, too, had to leave the field after receiving a very nasty kick to the head and came very close to losing his 'proboscis'. The other Pontypridd half, Bridge Merry, was also forced to concede a knockout blow from one of the Harlequin men, and several other of the 'Rhone' men showed unmistakable signs of deep mourning in and around the region of the peepers. An exciting first half saw the 'Quins leading by a drop-goal by Nicholls. After the restart, the visiting forwards, headed by Ack Llewellin, Bill Williams and Ivor Howells, distinguished themselves until they were severely handicapped when Rowlands left the field, and even more so when Christmas Jones also retired injured. Christmas was not so seriously injured as Gus Rowlands, but his nose looked like that of a pugilist. Despite this, Cardiff Harlequins could only add another try to their score in the second half, which left them victors by one drop goal and a try to nil (7-0). Pontypridd had every right to bemoan their luck, for fate was undoubtedly against them. To run the powerful Harlequins so close on their own ground with practically thirteen men ranked amongst their best performances of the season. They had a great deal more of the game than the score suggested, and were to be congratulated on their plucky stand. At forward, they were just as good as the home pack, while at half, Jones and Merry drew applause from the spectators. Ben Tiley had rarely played a better game at centre and was continually called upon to collar, which he seldom failed to do, and kicked magnificently. The burly schoolmaster generally played a very sound game against the Harlequins. Netherway, the substitute for Alun Morgan at fullback, was rather nervous and although his tackling was fair, he once or twice almost let the home lot in by his weak returns.

Christmas With Poor Vision!

It was unfortunate that Pontypridd were unable to field a full compliment of men for the away match at Neath on December 12th 1891, Alf Lewis, Ben Tiley, Francis Miles, Matt Nicholas and Bill Williams, being the most notable absentees. The game was not one to wax eloquently about, the black brigade winning by a penalty goal and four ties to nil (11-0).

Pontypridd did not have a sniff in the initial portion of the game and it was only one or two occasions that they were able to get beyond the equatorial line. The forwards, considering their weakened position, played as well as could be expected. The skipper, Ack Llewellin, Bowers, Watkins and Howells, all did a lot of work, the latter being particularly brilliant in the loose. Bill John, and Harry Davies worked hard, while veteran, Eddie Gould, who is always ready to turn out for his old club, donned the colours with credit to himself and his team. At half, Jack Ewans and Bridge Merry got along splendidly, though the stubby figure of Christmas Jones was sorely missed, he not having got over being kicked in the head in the previous match. He was, however, well enough to officiate on the touchline, in which he rendered his team splendid service! Perhaps the blow he had received has affected his vision, but certain it is that he was not particular to a few yards in this game. Alun Morgan, the custodian, had again returned like the prodigal son, and with the right royal welcome he received, he treated us to some of his old form.

Pontypridd Break The Whip On Cardiff's Back!

For eight long weeks Pontypridd had not won a match, their best achievement during this time being a draw with Llandaff, and for Pontypridd to break the whip on Cardiff's back, must certainly be dotted down as amongst the unforeseen, but this is exactly what they did!

The match was one of the fastest ever played on the park, the excitement being at fever pitch from first to last. The start was sensational in the extreme. Bert Taylor kicked off for the visitors, the oval falling into the hands of Pontypridd's Alf Lewis, whose kick was charged down, the leather bouncing back to within a few feet of the home line, where it was fought desperately until the home pack managed to sweep down the field to the visitors 25. The game for the next fifteen minutes waged here, there and everywhere, until Jack Davies, picking up from a dribble about twelve yards from the Cardiff line, dashed over with a fine try amidst vociferous cheering. A breathless silence reigned whilst Ben Tiley took the place kick, but the ball went wide. After this, the 'Blue and Blacks' pulled themselves together but to no earthly purpose, and round after round of applause rent the air when Jim Enoch fell across the rubicon for the second Pontypridd try, but the conversion was another failure.

After lemon time, the home men, playing with characteristic spirit, carried the cowhide into the visitors 25, where veteran, Ben Tiley, received and going like a locomotive scored the try of the day almost under the crossbar, Alun Morgan converting. After this, the home side fell away and Hill got over in the corner for Cardiff after a fine run, Bert Taylor failing with the kick. It was all over then and the hostilities ceased, leaving Pontypridd victors by one goal and three tries to one try (or 11-2).

The home forwards had never been seen to such advantage, and literally rushed the visitors off their legs. 'Old Evergreen', Bill Williams, played like a true Briton and Ivor Howells showed brilliant form, his pace serving him splendidly. The skipper, Ack Llewellin, led his men in fine style and did grandly in the line-outs. Ray Watkins put in all he knew, and Harry Davies collared and dropped his men in no halfhearted manner. Jim Enoch proved himself a hard worker, and justified his place in the front ranks. The halves, Bridge Merry and Christmas Jones, seemed to understand each other better, and gave the Cardiff pair a warm time of it. Ben Tiley was the best centre, head and shoulders above the others, his try being a scorcher. Ben Lewis did a lot of good work, his tall kicks helping his team to an immeasurable extent. Left wing, Walter J Davies, played a champion game, but Alf Lewis on the other wing had few chances. Alun Morgan, at fullback, displayed a talent in goal beyond all praise. 'Toricus' in the Glamorgan Free Press the following week wrote:

'Oh! What a surprise! Good old Cardiff came down 'flop' on Taff Vale Park on the first Saturday of the new year. One Cardiff correspondent wrote: "There was joy in the camp of the Pontypriddians on Saturday night" but he couldn't have been there, for he would not have called it joy, for that's no name for it, for the players and spectators were "Jimmy-fair-cracked-gone-mad!" and no wonder either. However, the accounts of the match given by some unprejudiced (?) Cardiff newspapers were really amusing: "A scratchy scratchy lot" said one referring to Cardiff, or "Only four regular men", said another and from the most odious of excuses, this one takes the cake: "It was just a shadow of its ancient glory that Cardiff took to Pontypridd". Is it any small wonder the "Rhone's" get disheartened when such prejudiced reports get into the press? It is not insinuated that Cardiff were fully represented, but it was known before the match that they could not field a full side, as the international match at Stradey Park was the same day. As it happens, however, the match committee of the Welsh Union thought it wise to only select one member of the Cardiff team, that being the champion wing, Pearson. Pontypridd were assuredly not to blame for the absence of Biggs, Fitzgerald and Escott, and were heartily sorry for the inability of the visitors to play their strongest team.'

Morriston Raced Off Their Feet

Pontypridd travelled to West Wales on January 23rd 1892, to face Morriston, and were minus their captain, Ack Llewellin, who was slightly indisposed. The wearers of the 'Rhone' were anxious to a degree to avenge the defeat that they had suffered on their own soil earlier in the season. How far they succeeded is now a matter of almost ancient history, for, after a hard game, they landed home just three points ahead of Morriston. The game was stubborn, the homesters having a big pull in the avoirdupois side of the question, but were in no way to be compared to the visitors in the point of ability, the 'Rhone' forwards fairly racing them off their feet. On their own confession, they were fairly beaten and can thank Dame Fortune that they did not suffer a crushing defeat, as Ben Tiley scored a try that was not allowed, and Alf Lewis all but scored, the ball going into touch-in-goal. It must have been evident to all that the score of one goal to Pontypridd and one try to Morriston (2-5) at the final whistle, in no way related to the respective merits of the two teams, and to qualify these statements, during the first half the homesters did not on one single occasion find their way over the equatorial line.

Two Heavy Engagements

Pontypridd fulfilled two heavy home engagements in four days. The first, on a Saturday, January 30th 1892, was billed as the struggle for the championship of the Rhondda, against Penygraig, which ended 0-0, but if minors were to count, Pontypridd emerged winners by four to three. In the second match on Tuesday, February

2nd, they came out second best to Wakefield Trinity by one try to nil (0-2) after a grandly contested game.

In both matches, the Pontypriddians were handicapped in point of weight, but especially in the latter, the Trinitarians being veritable giants. Apart from this, there was nothing very striking about them, their play partaking of a very reckless character. They were far removed from being adept at the passing game, though they played very unselfishly, but the manner in which they threw the 'hide' about was, at times, ridiculous.

Fairly Beaten At Aberavon

When Pontypridd visited Aberavon on February 13th 1892, the game from a spectators point of view was a 'frost', being confined for the major part to the forwards. As it was, it was here that the home men had the pull and a decidedly big pull too. This was all the more surprising because much had been heard of late about the Pontypridd pack, who although light, had hitherto proved themselves most resourceful, and though often beaten in the tight, they had always managed to make a furious pace for their opponents in the open play. On this day, however, they were beaten in both tight and loose. Seldom, if ever, did they bring off one of those dribbles for which they had become noted, and as one account put it "to put it mildly, they seemed as fairly crook as they were fairly beaten". If their forwards could have held their own, there is no doubt that Pontypridd could have pulled it off, but as it was they were defeated by one drop goal and one try to nil (8-0).

Gus Still Injured

By mid-February, Gus Rowlands, the Pontypridd centre threequarter, who was injured against Cardiff Harlequins on December 5th 1891, was apparently still unable to play or work. One local newspaper reported:

'Gus Rowlands' benefit match promises to be a huge success. The name of the opposing team has not yet been published, but I am assured that it will consist of Cardiff talent. Maritime decided a week ago to do their best to make the match a success by refusing a home fixture against the Welsh Wanderers - a team of selected players. A counter attraction of that kind would have proved a thorn in the side of the benefit, and the Maritime committee are to be complimented on showing a magnanimous feeling which should tend to produce something like harmony between the Pontypridd and Maritime clubs 'so near and yet so far'.'

Maritime At Stradey Park

Meanwhile, the Maritime Colliery team had secured an important fixture by playing in Llanelly on March 3rd 1892. This was the first time that these teams had met, so the visitors were an unknown quantity for the Scarlets, but by the end of the game had earned respect from their opponents. The match report that was written by "Collar Low" in the Llanelly and County Guardian seems to show that the match went on for hours. It read:

'There were rival attractions on Saturday, and as a newspaper man I examined both very carefully before I fixed upon my choice. There was Mabon (The South

Wales Miners Leader - Ed.) at the seaside and Maritime at Stradey - which was it to be? After two hours anxious thought and impartial consideration, I took the football engagement, justifying my choice by the fact that although I had heard Mabon many a time I had never in my life witnessed the prowess of the jerseyed heroes of Maritime. Another newspaper man who had made the same choice withered me up with a glance for looking upon the matter in the light I had, observing with inimitable unction that if he had seen Maritime a score of times and Mabon never, he would still have unhesitatingly selected the former, and let the Rhondda champion pass by. "Football hath charms indeed." So saith the enthusiast and so say I. By the way, we had our money's worth on Saturday. I had three hours of it myself and although the warfare was everything that the warmest footballer could desire, I drew the line at quarter to six and cleared off. Many won't believe it, I know, but it is true notwithstanding, football can be overdone.

A very big crowd assembled to witness the first appearance of the Maritime heroes upon the historic ground of Stradey, and when the match was over I was not the only man who regretted that the strangers had not been here before. Some of those not present at the match - and of course some enthusiasts were absent though the gate was what I would call a "flourishing" one - may think it a rash statement, but I must ask them to take upon trust, and that is that the Maritime men are as smart and clever a lot as I have seen at Stradey this season. Personally, I was mightily surprised and came away from the scene of conflict with a very keen sense of the merits of the visitors.

What went ye out to see? Just this, a second edition of the Penygraig encounter, one in which we would undoubtedly prove to be miles ahead of our opponents and one at the close of which, we should be leading by a few goals and as many tries, together with as many minors as goals and tries combined. But what a surprise, from start to finish the visitors were every bit worth as much as we were. Our fellows tried to give them the slip two or three times, but the "try again" business never blossomed into the promised fruition. The Maritime men refused to be left behind, and right to the finish they kept closely at our heels, not to speak of the occasional threat to outdo and to outdistance us.

Both teams were, broadly speaking well represented. With the slope in their favour during the first half, the visitors gave our men a pretty hot time of it, and I was among those who counted themselves lucky when at the call of half time we had a clean sheet. Changing ends, I was distinctly disposed to believe that we would be able to do the needful and put on another win to swell the record; but it was a delusive hope, for as the game proceeded with the home attempts to give the argument a decisive settlement, it became perfectly clear that the visitors had not come down to make themselves look silly, for playing up with such dash and determination that showed that they were not new to the work, but that their noviciate had been served a long time since, they not only kept our men out but once or twice had narrow shaves in jumping in. Ending eventually in a 0-0 draw, I confess that having regard to the character of the game, I was not all disappointed with the result.

Their forwards struck me as being an exceedingly fine lot, and it cannot for one moment be questioned that they distinctly had the pull over our fellows. They wheeled a treat and what is of infinite importance in such tactics, they never rollicked away without the ball. Practically beaten up front, it was consequently anything but plain sailing for the home halves, but the men in the third rank; considering the disadvantages, did amazingly well. Foster and Sullivan, on the other side, were albeit exceedingly smart, and won very warm encomiums from the crowd. Behind the scrum they had in Murray an extremely smart man, while his colleagues were by no means far behind.'

Final score: Llanelly 0 Maritime 0.

Cardiff Get Revenge

On March 5th 1892, Cardiff gained ample revenge for their defeat earlier in the season by beating Pontypridd at Cardiff Arms Park by one goal and three tries to nil (11-0). 'Marcus' in the Pontypridd Chronicle commented:

'So much has been written of this match that the efforts of my correspondence will appear rather second hand to the eager admirers of Ack Llewellin and his men. How often do we hear of a team being "beaten but not disgraced" and yet this is poor consolation at the best. I won't attempt to assert that Pontypridd should have beaten their formidable opponents, but one must admit

that the Cardiff team are not what they used to be, and just now are very low in the football ladder. Pontypridd supporters went mad when their pets secured a runaway victory over Cardiff at Taff Vale Park on the day of the international match but when I suggested that Cardiff were poorly represented, the reply that only a couple of the backs were away, was promptly tendered. Well, were Cardiff fully represented for this game? I think not, both wing men being away made a lot of difference to the Cardiff men I can assure you, especially when they happen to be the best in Wales. What I want to point out is the inconsistency of soundly thrashing them up here, and then to go down there and get beaten pointless by a team which was not fully representative. That is fair and good logic I believe.

Some say - but I do not know with what foundation - that the referee was rather inclined to partiality. Be that as it may, it is a wretchedly bad excuse and I don't agree with it. I have seldom seen anything but fair play given to both sides on Cardiff Arms Park. It is also astonishing how Pontypridd fullback, Alun Morgan, drops off in these big matches. His play was rather second rate. Ben Tiley and Benny Lewis were the pick of the Ponty quarters, and Bridge Merry was rather better than Christmas Jones at half, who held the ball far too long. Ack Llewellin and Bill Williams were the pick of the forwards, who more than held their own. The home team, however, were altogether more quicker on the ball, and it was in this way that they held such an advantage that led to victory.'

Penarth Fairly Puzzled

Pontypridd surprised their supporters with a marvellous display in a home match against Penarth on March 12th 1892, by two tries to nil (4-0). Alun Morgan played brilliantly at back, his kicking being superb and his tackling very secure. Ben Tiley and Benny Lewis, shared the honours at threequarter, and the defence of the whole quartet was splendid. Of the forwards there was nothing but praise, the way in which they heeled the scrums fairly puzzled the Penarthians, their rushing and dribbling being a treat and because everyone played so well, it would have been invidious to single out anyone for praise.

Crossing Of Swords

The biggest gate of the season assembled at Taff Vale Park on March 19th 1892, to witness what had anxiously been looked forward to as the match of the season, the crossing of swords between the far fabled Scarlet Runners of Llanelly, and Pontypridd. In view of the exceedingly fine form exhibited by the home lot against Penarth, backers of the 'Rhone' lads were exceptionally sanguine as to the result, at any rate, it was thought that even if the 'Tinopolitans' did manage to pull it off, it would only be by a small margin. But alas! Pontypridd once more deceived their supporters, the result going in favour of the Western lads by two goals and one try to nil (0-12).

It is needless to remark that the Pontypriddians were disappointed, but to say so was putting it mildly. Disappointment reigned supreme in the camp of the homesters, where there was much weeping, wailing and gnashing of teeth with a vengeance, and small wonder either. But why the lamentations? Why because the followers of the home team had become inebriated with the glorious victory of their pets over Penarth, and they had been building up such lofty castles in the air, that for the foundations to be shattered in such a rude fashion, for all their lofty structures to come tumbling down at one fell stroke, why the levelling of the walls of Jericho could not be compared to this result! But it is true that the final score was by no means indicative of the respective merits of the two teams. The packs were well matched, Pontypridd holding a slight advantage here; of the halves, however. the same old tale must be told, beaten and badly beaten, about that there is no mistake. Of course, they were opposed by a pair that could be reckoned upon as the warmest halves in the principality, but that was no excuse of the miserably feeble showing of the home pair. Beaten at half, the threequarters had little to do in the aggressive, and when they did bring something off, it was entirely of their own making. Hardly once throughout the game did the halves get the ball right away to the centres, and when they did, they either gave it away carelessly or tried to give it to the farthest away, thereby losing a lot of valuable time and ground. A B Evans gave splendid service on the wing, while Ben Tiley was a source of constant annoyance to his opponents. Ben Lewis seemed in his element on the right wing, his really good exhibition, however, was marred by one fatal mistake, which let in Lovering to score.

Amongst the home pack, Bill Williams and Ack Llewellin shone most. Bowers and Harry Davies did exceedingly well and Jim Enoch was evident throughout. Clapp was brought in for Walter Davies, who played on the left wing, the latter holding a watching brief over Percy Lloyd, never once letting the Llanelly flyer become dangerous. Matt Nicholls, however, still played to the gallery and as the Pontypridd pack could not afford to carry any passengers, many thought it advisable that the match committee should see that he gets down to share of the donkey work, or throw him out. At fullback, Alun Morgan was in fine form and saved his side from disaster on several occasions. His kicking partook of a Leviathan order, and the way in which he stopped the ugly rushes of the Llanelly forwards was a treat. Harry Stead, of the Maritime Colliery team stepped in to fill a vacancy in the home pack, and did well in the open, but did not enhance his reputation as a scrummager.

Maltese Cross Boys Defeated

There was a good muster around the ropes at Taff Vale Park on March 26th 1892 for the visit of Neath, but not as many the number as the previous week when Llanelly were the visitors, the defeat in that game mitigating against what would otherwise have been a roaring gate. Despite the Llanelly defeat, there were still plenty of sturdy Pontypriddians who were prepared to stake a little bet on their pets, their idea being that the defeat was by no means to be taken as a fair index of the form of the 'Rhone' lads. That they were justified in their belief is amply demonstrated by the result of this encounter with the 'Maltese Cross' boys because Neath were defeated by the tune of one goal and two tries to one drop goal and one try (9-7).

There was no disputing that Pontypridd were well beaten at forward. It was not that often that there was much fault to be found with the pack, indeed, it was questionable whether this display could be called a 'fault', for they tried their level best. Still, they were whacked and unmistakingly so. The presence of Hill was immensely felt, he being by far the best halfback that had played for Pontypridd this season and though some do not believe in bringing in strangers, the selection committee did well in securing him for this match. His confrere, however, did not shine as brightly, but this was due to the fact that he invariably played the scrums, while Hill stood out. Of the quarters, Cooper scored a splendid try and the way in which he did it was truly marvellous. Taking a pass from Hill in splendid style, he got going like a racehorse and just as everyone thought he would be pushed into touch, he put his foot on the ball, then using his sprinting powers in good fashion, he fielded it just as it dropped, and got clean round, scoring one of the prettiest tries ever scored on the field. A B Evans also scored a try, the reward for a dashing sprint in which he fairly beat the opposing backs. Benny Lewis did admirably on the wing, which appears to be his proper place. He has played in every position except forward, but nowhere has he done so well as on the wing.

Double Programme

On March 30th 1892, Pontypridd prepared a double programme, Pontypridd Juniors v Pontypridd 'A' at

3.30pm and Pontypridd v Treorchy at 4.30; all for a 'Blooming Tanner!' Two sides so strictly local as Pontypridd and Treorchy brought a fair gate, and the weather was just lovely. Seeing that Maritime had beaten Treorchy by twenty points to nil, it was thought that Pontypridd had an easy thing going, but they were mistaken, and although the visitors were beaten by one goal to nil (5-0), they had the consolation of knowing that they had had quite as much of the play as the winning team. Perhaps the wheeling of the home pack was cleverer at the start of the game but a tremendous lot of hard pushing and deadly tackling by the visiting eight soon rubbed this off the home lot, and left them with nothing to spare. The match, however, was not an interesting one. One incident occurred, however, which every sportsman and footballer will sincerely regret, which was the accident that befell A B Evans, the home centre, which will certainly deprive the team of his services for some time. This could not have happened at a more inopportune time, for if ever the 'Rhone' lads require to be well and strongly represented, it would be next Saturday when they crossed swords with the Cardiff Harlequins.

Against Treorchy, Jim Connelly (Maritime) assisted the visitors at fullback, and the way the home spectators jeered him for a slip or two, clearly demonstrated the bad feeling that exists between the supporters of both clubs. 'Marcus' in the Pontypridd Chronicle commented:

'The rapid strides which football in the district around Pontypridd has made in the last few years is astonishing. Look back about four years when our

Winter pastime was played with more or less success by several scratch organisations, such as the Chainworks Rovers, Pontypridd Juniors, Taff Vale Wanderers and the Maritime Colliery team just starting, with our position now, with two of the best second class clubs in the principality. But there is not sufficient room in the town for two such teams, and we should have only one. The result would be a better team, larger gates and consequently a better lot of fixtures, which would open the eyes of the community to its true value as a physical recreation.'

More Chasing Of The Inflatable Cowhide

'Old Sol' shone forth in all his glory for the home game against Cardiff Harlequins on April 4th 1892, it being more suitable for 'the manipulation of the willow' than for the chasing of the 'inflated cowhide', in an ordeal these two teams went through on the Taff Vale Park. Probably with the idea of giving the atmospherical condition time to undergo the cooling process, the kick off was timed for 4pm. This was a good move, and clearly showed the considerate nature of the leading lights of the Pontypridd club, who to all appearances, did not wish to see their pets 'boiled in their own fat'.

The home team were decidedly unfortunate in the loss of A B Evans, injured in the Treorchy game, and added to this, they were compelled by sheer force of circumstances to requisition the services of two halves, Christmas Jones and Bridge Merry, who they had previously thrown out; there again, they were also minus a regular forward, but nothing was made of this, for the veteran, Eddie Gould, stepped forward to fill the break, so that in this instance Pontypridd were better off for the change. Taken altogether, it cannot be held that the chances of the home team were bright, in fact, there were many of the 'thick and thin' supporters of Pontypridd, who were inclined to be a little down in the dumps as to the result.

The match itself was well fought out, but it was not by any means a brilliant exposition of the game, probably under the meteorological conditions the players felt more like "necking" than "kicking". Between the two packs there was not a lot to choose, the visitors were bigger and heavier here, and did alright in the scrums, though often they brought off a "wheel" without the ball, thus giving the homesters several chances, of which they availed themselves. The home halves were not of the effulgent order, the visiting pair being most resourceful, but to talk to the frequenters of the Taff Vale Park of the capabilities of the home couple would be to commit an almost unpardonable error. The threequarters were well met, while at forward the honours went to Bill Williams, Eddie Gould and Matt Nicholls. The last named player did not have a very strong reputation as a scrummager, but in this game he did better than he has ever done before.

Ben Lewis played a champion game on the wing. His attempt at goal was a truly marvellous effort, and nine out of ten spectators assembled, would have sworn that the oval had crossed over the crossbar from his drop kick. However, the referee ruled otherwise, and there it must rest. Ben Tiley proved a cunning centre, while Jimmy Green, the other centre, drafted in from the 'A' team, was certainly a "warm 'in' but many thought he should be tried at half, a position in which they think he will cover himself in glory. Winger, Walter Davies, held a watching brief over 'Quins international, Fred Nicholls, who was never allowed to get away. Of the Harlequins pack, Coles and Phillips were the best. Bennett, however, would be the best forward imaginable if talking constituted a good player!

'Marcus' in the Pontypridd Chronicle was highly critical of some of the home supporters in his match report the following week, and wrote:

'I was greatly disappointed in this game, although it was fast and well contested, it was rather too rough to be enjoyable. The 'Quins forwards made no mistake when they held a man. If one couldn't floor his opponent, the whole pack would pounce upon him. Yet this is the team, when the Maritime engaged their attention in Cardiff, left the field with the ejaculation: "Well, if this is Maritime, then they are a rough lot". Great Snakes! And to hear a team like the 'Quins talk about roughness, well, well! there are some strange incongruities in football!

I cannot say I admire the manner in which our spectators gave vent to their feelings in the second half towards the referee. I believe everyone who understands the question will agree with me that there is no better judge of the game in Wales, and no gentleman with a keener desire to do justice to both sides than Mr Gwynn. Several times, however, his decisions gave rise to a perfect howl from the spectators on the riverside side of the field. Now, if this sort of thing becomes the rule, it is not the spectators who will suffer, but the club. Notices have already been posted at various grounds cautioning spectators against treating the referees of the union in such an ungentlemanly manner, and I should be very sorry to see our club on the suspended list. So Beware! Ye spectators, and bottle up your anger against referees. It is an unenviable position as a referee and one I should not care about, still, I have had the misfortune, or the weakness, whichever you like - of blowing the whistle once this season and although I did my best, was soundly blown up occasionally by the losing side. Of course, I didn't care whether they liked it or not. I thought I was doing right, and stuck to my decisions with the strong conviction that they really were.'

A Good Finish

The Pontypridd Club concluded its second season after reforming, with home victories over Aberdare, Kent Wanderers and Abergavenny Wanderers, but due to local elections and bank holidays, they went unreported.

On April 29th 1892, the Pontypridd Chronicle carried the following reports:

Football by 'Marcus'

A Review Of The Season
- The Amalgamation Question

With last Saturdays game between Maritime and Cardiff Harlequins, the 1892 football season closes as far as the principal teams of Pontypridd are concerned. The Maritime team which journeyed to Cardiff to fulfil this last fixture, was a very strong one and indeed was almost the best we could turn out under any circumstances. Alun Morgan and Ben Tiley, of Pontypridd, assisted the colliers behind, and Eddie Gould took the place of Tom Harry at forward. The result, a try each (2-2) was not only satisfactory to the Maritime team, but also serves to show that the proposed amalgamation accomplished, we could put on the field a team strong enough to "take the rise" out of even the 'Quins on their own ground, a fact which the best teams in the principality would find hard to accomplish. I mean by this, of course, that if we take the result of the Maritime season as a criterion to gauge the abilities of a new amalgamation, and granting that we could improve Saturdays team by three points, that would be sufficient to place us on a substantial footing in first class company. No doubt there would be some quibbling at first as to the selection of the best team, but in the end I should think the following players would make a combination which would thoroughly represent the strength of the district:

Alun Morgan(P)*

Steve Vickers(M) Ben Dickenson(M) Ben Tiley(P) Jack Murray(M)

Steve Sullivan(M) Tudor Foster(M)

O Bowers(M) Harry Stead(M) Jimmy Connelly M) Bill Williams(P) Patsy Devereaux(M)

Jack Hope M) Tom Hemsworth(M) Tom Murray(M)

*(P) = Pontypridd (M) = Maritime

This would be my selection, with the first reserve place being allotted to Ben Lewis, Pontypridd, as centre threequarter. Many Pontypridd supporters would undoubtedly take exception to the preponderance of Maritime men in the forwards, but to anyone who understands forward play, and will view the question from an impartial standpoint, it is obvious that I have mentioned in the above side the cream of both teams. We have in Bowers, Hope, Devereaux and Tom Murray, four genuine hard workers, which are absolutely necessary in a pack. Stead, Williams, Connelly and Hemsworth, are all splendid men in the open and I think taken all round, the forwards mentioned would constitute a pack able to beat nine out of every ten teams in Wales. The Maritime halves are admittedly a warm pair, and I don't think we could improve on them in the district. Murray and Vickers are, in my opinion, our best wings, while Tiley and Dickenson are both good feeders, a quality which is essential in centres. Alun Morgan, is undoubtedly the coming fullback in Wales and would be the selection of both parties.

The only obstacle now, so rumours say, in way of the amalgamation scene seems to be the question of which ground will be used. Candidly, I think Maritime should give way on this point, but the Pontypriddians should bear in mind that Maritime will be giving up a title by which they have considerably honoured during the season ending this week, and will also be supplying two-thirds of the players. The Taff Vale Park has the best entrance and appointments, but the quality of the turf is nothing to fuss over, as we could soon have either returfed. A committee consisting of an equal number from each club should be appointed, and the other officials should work harmoniously together. In the event of forming an Athletic and Football Club, it should be simple enough to start a much needed gymnasium, and who knows what, in a few seasons, we could produce a record similar to the Usksiders. So much for the amalgamation, before this reaches the eyes of the public, the question will be settled one way or another. The sooner the better I say!'

Pontypridd - opened their season with a creditable victory over Newport Harriers, followed by a hard tussle with Cardiff Stars. In this game Pontypridd scored a lucky win from a try obtained by Alf Lewis, after the ball had rebounded from a tree on the lower side of the field. The Llanelly match proved disastrous to the 'Rhone' lads, a twenty-two points to two defeat being the extent of their drubbing at the hands of the 'Tinplaters'. Another reverse awaited them on the following Saturday from Morriston, who beat them by two goals to nil. In the ensuing matches with Merthyr, Caerphilly, Splott Rovers and Cardiff University, they scored four wins, with eighty-five points to nothing in their favour. Then came the most disastrous month of the season, matches being lost successively with Penygraig, Penarth, Pontymister, Cardiff Harlequins and Neath. A draw with Llandaff and a more sensational victory over Cardiff, followed by a success at Morriston, once more gained the confidence of the supporters, but the team then performed in a very in-and-out fashion until their encounter with Penarth, who they vanquished by three tries to nothing. Llanelly were fortunate in winning their fixture, and Pontypridd had a large share of what luck was knocking about the day they beat Neath. Two victories over Merthyr and Treorchy came next, Cardiff 'Quins being the last team to beat the representatives of the town club. Notwithstanding the absence of one or two good players through injuries, three victories over Aberdare, Kent Wanderers and Abergavenny, wound up the season with a flourish. Financially, the season has been a fair one and I believe that I am right in saying that the club will come through it all right. Much credit is due to Mr Edward Llewellin, the Honorary Secretary of the club, whose efforts are much appreciated by players and supporters alike.

Maritime - Never in the history of the Maritime club has so much success attended the efforts of the players as during the season just ended. Their opponents at the commencement of the season were one after the other disposed of easily, and in the first dozen matches or so they defeated pointless, with the exception of Aberavon, who dropped a goal, Treorchy, Swansea 'A', Aberavon, Grangetown and District, Ton Rangers, Skewen, Morriston, Tondu, Ystrad, Llandaff and St Davids.

Not a very strong list some may say, but it must be borne in mind that Morriston and Aberavon were just then playing a warm game. Then, the match against Llandaff came as a surprise to supporters of the team, but it was not until this match that the Maritime line was crossed. Penarth next visited Maesycoed, and were fortunate in getting off with a try each, although the weather could not permit a continuation of the game after halftime. Aberavon was the next team visited, and a victory by a point over one of the strongest second class teams of the season. A draw with Morriston and a victory over such old enemies as Penygraig, prefaced the tour through Yorkshire, which was highly gratifying to the club.

Cardiff Stars were next defeated and an exhibition game with Cardiff Harlequins was followed by a game with the same team the following Saturday, the 'Quins winning by three tries to nothing. A lose at Penarth was followed by the defeating of Treorchy, St Davids, Penygraig and away draws with such crack organisations as Gloucester and Llanelly. Swansea 'A' and Penygraig then beat them on successive Saturdays but victories were not yet done with, and the Welsh Wanderers, Splott Rovers, Penygraig and Tondu were all defeated. Armley caught them in a losing mood, and then the season was wound up with a draw at Cardiff Harlequins. A successful season has now been brought to a close and the supporters and management must be satisfied with the performance of the team. The duties of Secretary, have been ably carried out by Mr S Humphreys, who has been indefatigable in his efforts to place the team on a substantial footing in good company, and deserves the hearty thanks of all connected with the club.

And so the second season of the Pontypridd Club had come to an end. On the field, things had gone fairly well but obviously they still appeared a little weak at forward and at half but Ack Llewellin must still have been justifiably proud of the club record at the end of the season. It appeared that by the end of April 1892, secret talks had already been held on the amalgamation of the two premier teams in the town but would this cloak and dagger stuff lead to a happy conclusion? We will find out in our next chapter.

Pontypridd RFC - Results Season 1891-92

1891

Date	Opponent	Venue	For G	For T	Against G	Against T	Result
Sept 19th	Newport Harriers	Home	0	3	0	1	Won
Sept 26th	Cardiff Stars	Away	1	1	0	2	Won
Oct 3rd	Llanelly	Away	0	1	4	1	Lost
Oct 10th	Morriston	Home	0	0	2	0	Lost
Oct 12th	Merthyr	Home	3	2	0	0	Won
Oct 17th	Caerphilly	Home	1	5	0	0	Won
Oct 24th	Splott Rovers	Home	2	0	0	0	Won
Oct 27th	Cardiff University	Home	5	8	0	0	Won
Oct 31st	Penygraig	Away	0	0	0	1	Lost
Nov 7th	Penarth	Away	0	0	1	2	Lost
Nov 14th	Pontymister	Home	0	0	1	2	Lost
Nov 28th	Aberavon	Home	Postponed				
Dec 5th	Cardiff Harlequins	Away	0	0	1	1	Lost
Dec 12th	Neath	Away	0	1	0	1	Draw
Dec 19th	Llandaff	Home	0	1	0	1	Draw
Dec 25th	Newport Harriers	Away	Postponed				
Dec 26th	Kendal	Home	Postponed				

1892

Date	Opponent	Venue	For G	For T	Against G	Against T	Result
Jan 2nd	Cardiff	Home	1	2	0	2	Won
Jan 23rd	Morriston	Away	1	0	0	1	Won
Jan 30th	Penygraig	Home	0	0	0	0	Draw
Feb 2nd	Wakefield Trinity	Home	0	0	0	1	Lost
Feb 6th	Caerphilly	Home	1	5	0	0	Won
Feb 13th	Aberavon	Away	0	0	1	1	Lost
Feb 27th	Aberavon	Home	0	1	0	1	Draw
Mar 5th	Cardiff	Away	0	1	1	3	Lost
Mar 12th	Penarth	Home	0	2	0	0	Won
Mar 19th	Llanelly	Home	0	0	2	1	Lost
Mr 26th	Neath	Home	1	2	1	1	Won
Mar 28th	Merthyr	Away	0	4	0	0	Won
Mar 30th	Treorchy	Home	1	0	0	0	Won
Apr 4th	Cardiff Harlequins	Home	0	0	1	0	Lost
Apr 10th	Aberdare	Home	1	3	0	0	Won
Apr 11th	Kent Wanderers	Home	1	2	0	0	Won
Apr 13th	Abergavenny Wanderers	Home	1	2	-0	0	Won

G = Converted Try T = Try

Captain First XV, Ack Llewellin; Vice Captain, Francis Miles; Second XV Captain, Reuben Richards; Vice Captain, Tom Evans; President, James Roberts; Ground, Taff Vale Park; Secretary, Edward Llewellin; Treasurer, Evan Williams; Headquarters, Sportsman Hotel; Overall Playing Record: P31, W16, L12, D3.

Maritime Colliery - Results Season 1891-92

1891

			For		Against		
			G	T	G	T	
Sept 19th	Treorchy	Away	2	5	0	0	Won
Sept 26th	Swansea 'A'	Away	2	4	0	0	Won
Oct 3rd	Aberavon	Home	0	3	1*	0	Won
Oct 7th	Grangetown District	Home	4	3	0	0	Won
Oct 10th	Ton Rangers (Ystrad)	Home	2	1	0	0	Won
Oct 17th	Skewen	Home	2	5	0	0	Won
Oct 24th	Morriston	Home	0	3	0	0	Won
Oct 31st	Tondu	Away	0	5	0	0	Won
Nov 3rd	Ystrad Excelsiors	Home	1	6	0	0	Won
Nov 7th	Llandaff	Home	0	1	0	0	Won
Nov 14th	St Davids (Cardiff)	Home	0	2	0	0	Won
Nov 21st	Llandaff	Away	0	0	0	1	Lost
Nov 28th	Penarth	Home	0	1	0	1	Draw
Dec 5th	Aberavon	Away	1	1	1*	1	Won
Dec 12th	Morriston	Away	0	0	0	0	Draw
Dec 19th	Penygraig	Home	0	1	0	0	Won
Dec 25th	Sowerby Bridge	Away	1	2	1	0	Won
Dec 26th	Mossley	Away	1	2	0	1	Won
Dec 28th	Shipley	Away	2	0	1	0	Won
Dec 30th	Wakefield Trinity	Away	0	3	3	0	Lost

1892

Jan 2nd	Cardiff Stars	Home	3	1	0	0	Won
Jan 16th	Cardiff Harlequins	Home	0	0	0	0	Draw
					(Exhibition game)		
Jan 23rd	Cardiff Harlequins	Home	0	0	0	3	Lost
Feb 6th	Penarth	Away	0	0	0	1	Lost
Feb 13th	Treorchy	Away	2	1	0	1	Won
Feb 17th	St Davids	Away	1	0	0	0	Won
Feb 20th	Penygraig	Away	1	0	0	0	Won
Mar 5th	Llanelly	Away	0	0	0	0	Draw
Mar 12th	Gloucester	Away	0	1	0	1	Draw
Mar 19th	Swansea 'A'	Away	0	0	0	1	Lost
Mar 26th	Penygraig	Away	0	1	1	0	Lost
Apr 4th	Welsh Wanderers	Home	2	1	0	1	Won
Apr 5th	Splott Rovers	Home	3	2	0	1	Won

Apr 9th	Penygraig	Home	1	0	0	0	Won
Apr 16th	Tondu	Home	2	4	0	1	Won
Apr 18th	Armley	Home	0	0	0	1	Lost
Apr 22nd	Cardiff Harlequins	Away	0	1	0	1	Draw

G = Converted Try T = Try * = Drop Goal

Captain, Benjamin Dickenson; Secretary, Mr S Humphreys; President, Mr Major Hague; Treasurer; Mr Holmes; Vice President, Dr Howard Davies; Ground, Maesycoed Field; Seasons Record: P37, W24, D6, L7.

CHAPTER THREE

AMALGAMATION COMPLETED
A NEW CLUB - A SUCCESSFUL SEASON

Where Shall We Play?

With the amalgamation of the Pontypridd and Maritime football clubs being within an ace of being brought about by the end of April 1892, the local newspapers openly discussed which field would be best, Taff Vale Park (Pontypridd) or the Maesycoed Field (Maritime), and one commented that the comfort of the spectators should be taken into consideration alongside those of the club and players. It was pointed out that the entrance to the Taff Vale Park was fairly good, while the access to the Maesycoed field was simply awful, and furthermore, there was no hope of improving it.

A would-be spectator wishing to get to the Maritime field had a few alternatives on how to arrive there. He, or she, had either to cross the top of the Maritime Pit, or scramble over the Barry Railway line. These were two shortcuts, but if a person wanted to walk along a road, they had either to trudge up to Newtown (Pwllgwaun) and come down on the field at Maesycoed, or attempt an ascent which was as steep as climbing the Alps by going up "the Rhiw" (Graig Hill) and descend into the valley by the lane by the Morning Star Hotel, wending their way past "the scene of many baptisms" and then onto the field.

Holdups "Blown Away"

A few weeks later, another meeting of the clubs was held to discuss the dispute over the field, the two already having agreed that the new club would be called:

THE PONTYPRIDD FOOTBALL
AND ATHLETIC CLUB

Those present at the meeting were:
Representing Maritime: Mr Major Hague (President), Mr Holmes (Treasurer) and Dr Howard Davies (Vice-President). Representing Pontypridd: Mr Edward Llewellin (Secretary), Mr Teddy Lewis (Chairman) and Mr Ack Llewellin (Captain).

The meeting got off to a bad start, the building in which it was held having its roof blown off in a high wind, and eventually they moved to the Maritime's team headquarters, The Rose and Crown Hotel, Graig. After a long discussion it was resolved that the final decision be left to the representatives of the Welsh Union, Mr Davies (Cardiff Harlequins), Mr Butler (Aberavon) and Mr Dewar (Penarth). In a subsequent visit to the town, the arbitrators decided that although the Taff Vale Park was not a model ground, it was least of two evils, and therefore the amalgamated club should play at Treforest.

There was an alternative though. It was hoped that the club could secure a field at Ynysangharad, which with a bit of work could be converted into one of the best grounds in the principality. The club hoped to persuade Lady Lanover's agent to rent a field to the club, and then the Welsh Union trial match planned for Pontypridd in

December, could be played there. However, even with such prominent men in the club such as Mr David Leyshon (Manager, Newbridge Brewery), Mr Major Hague (Agent of the Maritime Colliery) and Dr Howard Davies (Chief Medical Officer for the local board of health), they were unsuccessful, so Taff Vale Park it WOULD have to be.

With the amalgamation finally achieved, the followers of the two old teams, who for so long had waited to see their "pets" take their place amongst the leading Welsh clubs, were now satisfied that their most sanguine visions would soon be realised, and Pontypriddians, with a bound, would seize the proud position in the football world which internal dissension's alone, had prevented them from occupying. When it was remembered that when there were two organisations in the town, one of them, Pontypridd, had vanquished Cardiff and Neath last season, and the other, Maritime, had fought draws with such certified teams such as Gloucester and Llanelly, and had got the better of Penygraig three times out of four, the supporters of the new club would now be able to gauge the relative merits of the Pontypridd footballers against those of other towns. However, the task of choosing the first XV for the first match of the season would not be an easy one, and with so many players to choose from, the match committee would have to be composed of "gentlemen" in the real sense of the word. The Glamorgan Free Press give this view of who should be on the selection committee:

> 'They must not be like weather cocks, turning with every little breeze, they must have perfectly open

minds, and must not judge a man's abilities until they have seen him play. They must hold no personal grudges against any man, or at least if they do, as I suppose every man has his enemies, they must not on any consideration allow it to enter the committee room; all feelings towards any of the players, whether friendly or otherwise, must be left on the mat, or anywhere, as long as it does not interfere with their judgement; and above all, they must attend their duties; their Saturday afternoons must be spent a the football field, for only seeing the men play can they form their opinions. There are quite a number of such men available and foremost amongst them stands Mr Major Hague, Dr Howard Davies, Mr Holmes, Mr John Daniel Jones, Teddy Lewis and Mr E S Richards. The claim of these gentlemen will have to be discussed and whoever else might be elected, I think that with a committee composed of such men as these, we shall never again hear the cry of "bought for the price of a pint!" I will not upstage the functions of the match committee by naming a team. I would leave that to those selected to act when the time comes, and we know which players are available. I will content myself now with stating that I sincerely hope the amalgamation scheme, which has so amicably been contracted, will never again be departed from. Under these conditions Pontypridd will soon attain a proud position.'

With the amalgamation now complete, towards the start of the new season, the new club called a General Meeting. The balance sheet showed that both teams were in financial difficulties, and that the amalgamation was of mutual benefit to all.

Pontypridd Amalgamated Football and Athletic Club

First Annual General Meeting

Popular Appointments

The first annual meeting of the Pontypridd Football and Athletic club, was held on Saturday August 26th 1892, at the Victoria Hall and was presided over by Mr Major Hague. There was a large attendance.

Financial Report

Mr Edward Llewellin, the popular secretary of the late Pontypridd club, reported that the receipts for last season amounted to £162-8s-0d, and the expenses £200-3s-7d, leaving a balance to the bad of £37-15s-7d. This resulted from bad gates and irregularity on the part of subscribers and others. Mr Humphreys, the secretary of the late Maritime club, also stated that their club had a balance on the wrong side of £65, owing probably to the tour last season, which cost them about £75.

The Chairman's Address

Mr Major Hague, in the course of a splendid speech, said that he felt a great pleasure to meet the amalgamated club that evening under such favourable auspices (hear, hear). He hoped that the arrangements which had already been made, would be carried out and a really good club would be brought into existence, but this could only be done by the footballers working shoulder to shoulder. Then they would have a team equal to any in South Wales (cheers). They would have a lot of good players and by perseverance they ought to be able to turn out as good a fifteen as Cardiff or Newport (applause). They already had the stuff from which good players were made, and they only required practice and system to perfect them (hear, hear). The room in which they met, would be, in a short while, formed into a gymnasium and that, he believed, would be the making of the club (hear, hear). As far as the financial affairs stood, they could see that both the late clubs had balances on the wrong side and their difficulties had risen from the tour of Yorkshire when the weather and elements were against them, and being a club not popularly known, they did not obtain such gates as might have been expected. According to the fixture card for the ensuing season, however, he noticed that they were engaged to play some of the best teams of Yorkshire, and he believed that the team that would be sent from Pontypridd would hold its own very well (applause). He would do all that he could to support the club in every way. He flattered himself that he had done so at Maritime, where, when football was started they had but a poor show indeed. Since that time, however, matters had improved and he hoped to see some of the members this year getting their international caps (loud applause). In conclusion, he sincerely hoped that they would have a successful year, and if every member would do his best, he felt certain that that would be the case.

The New Heads

On the motion of Mr Edward Llewellin, seconded by Mr Major Hague, David Leyshon was unanimously elected president of the club for the ensuing year. Mr Llewellin moved, and Mr John Daniel Jones seconded, the election of Messrs James Roberts CC and Major Hague, as vice presidents. This was carried unanimously.

Election of Captain and Vice

Mr Ack Llewellin moved, and Mr Evan Williams seconded, the election of Mr Stephen Sullivan as captain of the first XV for the ensuing year. Mr Tom Hemsworth was also nominated, but on a vote being taken by ballot it was found that Mr Sullivan had been elected by forty four against fifteen accorded to Mr Hemsworth. Mr Alun Morgan was unanimously elected as vice-captain. Mr Sullivan, in returning thanks said that he felt proud of the position that he had this evening been appointed to, and felt certain that if he could in any way assist young players, he would at all times do so (hear, hear). He hoped before the end of the season to be able to captain a club second to none amongst the first class teams in Wales. Mr Alun Morgan having returned thanks for his election in suitable terms, Harry Stead, on behalf of Mr Tom Hemsworth, thanked the supporters of that gentleman, and stated that he felt certain Mr Hemsworth would still do his best for the good of the club (hear, hear).

The gentlemen nominated to lead the second fifteen were, namely, Messrs. James Lewis and G Seaton. On a vote being taken, however, Mr Lewis was declared elected by a majority of twenty-seven votes, and Mr Seaton was unanimously elected vice-captain.

Election Of Secretary And Treasurer

Three gentlemen were nominated to act as Treasurer for the ensuing year, namely, Messrs S Humphreys, W T Leyshon and W Holmes but the names of the latter two gentlemen were eventually withdrawn, and Mr Humphreys was elected unanimously.

Only one gentleman was nominated to fill the post of secretary, namely, the genial and ever popular Mr Ted Llewellin, who was elected unanimously amidst loud cheering. Mr Llewellin, in returning thanks, said that he was pleased with his reception and yet sad. Pleased because the club had shown that they still had confidence in him even after the cowardly attacks made upon him last season. In the past he had done his best for the team, and now that the two clubs were amalgamated, he felt that it would be a proud position for any man to hold (applause). He felt sad, however, to think that they had a balance on the wrong side, and, in fact, he would not have taken office this evening had the balance been on the right side, for he would like to leave the club with a good record and a clean sheet (loud applause).

Election Of The Committee

The following are the names of the gentleman nominated to act on the match committee to represent the Pontypridd club and the number of votes given each:

Elected: Ack Llewellin, 35; Teddy Lewis, 25; John Daniel Jones, 16. Not Elected: Eddie Gould, 13; Fred Edwards, 13; E Bowden, 4; D E Phillips, 4.

Messrs Hague, W Holmes and S Humphreys had already been elected to represent the Maritime club as part of the amalgamation agreement, as were Dr Howard Davies and Mr E S Richards.

The following were also elected to act as a general committee: Messrs E Bowden, J E James, E Sidbury, P Connelly, W Hague, R F Davies, Evan Williams, Thomas Edwards, A A Moreland, Hezekiah Hughes, Sgt A McDonald and D E Phillips. The usual vote of thanks to the chairman, moved by T E Lewis and seconded by Ack Llewellin, terminated the meeting.

The New Captain - A Biographical Sketch

Stephen Sullivan, who has been elected captain of the Pontypridd Amalgamated Football and Athletic Club for the season 1892-93, is a native of Neath, where he was born twenty-six years ago. He began taking an interest in the national game during the 1887-88 season, when he played for the Neath Institute. The following season he was elected to play for the premier team of the town, and took part in their matches against the prominent Cardiff and Llanelly teams. He moved to Pontypridd the following year, and immediately joined the late Maritime club, in which he was considered one of the best players since its foundation in season 1889-90. In the season of 1890-91, he became the captain of the Maritime team, and it may be mentioned that at this time the Maritime team became looked upon as one of the rising teams of South Wales, its rapid improvement being in great measure due to Sullivan's indefatigable exertions. He took great pains in teaching them the passing game for which the team became noted, and being an expert at the passing game himself, the popular captain soon made the members of his team adepts as well. Sullivan is a comparatively short, man but nevertheless is wiry and strong. He stands 5ft 7ins in height and weighs eleven stone, and according to all appearances he has this year every chance to lead on the new team to victory after victory, especially as he has by his side most of his old colleagues, of which great things are expected during the coming season.

A History Of Two Teams

With the new season rapidly approaching 'Vericus' in the Pontypridd Chronicle, gave a brief history of the former Pontypridd and Maritime clubs and a look to the future.

The Pontypridd club - was first formed in 1890-91, by the amalgamation of some Pontypridd players with the existing Treforest club, and although it has always borne a good name, there remains for it a far brighter future than has yet been imagined. Satisfactory progress was made last year although their play was not of even character throughout - the combination sometimes exhibiting excellent form, and at other times falling completely away. On the whole, however, the club carried through the season very creditably. Its chief exploit was conquering Cardiff by one goal and two tries to one try. Thirty one matches were played, sixteen of these were won, twelve lost, and three drawn. As is well known, Ack Llewellin made an excellent captain, and his brother Edward made one of the best football secretaries in south Wales. Always kind and obliging, he is respected by all and the players, who included Ben Tiley, Ben Lewis, Alun Morgan, Christmas Jones, Ivor Howells, and were fit successors to such men as William and James Spickett, D Jenkins and other old well known Pontypridd boys. At the end of the year the question of amalgamation with Maritime was broached with the result we all know. In future, Pontypridd will present a formidable combination of players to do battle in the football field for the honour of the metropolis of the East Glamorgan coalfield. The combined team have already acquired a hall for the purpose of converting it into a fully equipped gymnasium and the other concomitants of a sporting rendezvous.

The Maritime Club - also deserve a word of comment. The team owes its origin to the enterprise of a few enthusiastic football followers at the Maritime Colliery, prominent amongst whom were Mr Major Hague, the agent of the company; Mr Holmes, the Cashier; and Mr Humphreys, who acted as secretary to the club. These gentlemen secured the Mill Field, Pontypridd but had not occupied it more than three months when it was taken away from them. A club committee then approached Mr White, the principal director of the colliery, and succeeded in obtaining from him the use of the colliery field, which they levelled and at some expense put it into a fit condition for playing on. Tom Hemsworth was the club's first captain, a genial fellow and a stalwart player was "Tom". In their first season the modest little team took on the principal clubs of the district. They played one match with Penygraig and got knocked out by two goals and five tries. Such a thorough "dressing down" would have dampened the ardour of a less plucky contingent of players than the colliery boys, but this ignoble defeat only made them feel more determined to improve. Last season the tables were carefully turned, the Maritime winning three out of four matches with Penygraig, the points being Maritime fourteen, Penygraig four. In the second season Ben Dickenson captained them, and as a centre threequarter he now has few equals in the district. Stephen Sullivan succeeded to the captaincy in the third season and he was proved to be the most successful and most popular captain the Maritime had ever had. Stephen threw all his energy in the duties of his position and succeeded in affecting a rapid improvement in the team. Last season Ben Dickenson again took the reins, and the record for that period shows: Twenty four wins, six draws and seven losses. Among the drawn games were away matches with Llanelly and Gloucester.

At Christmas 1891, the team allowed its ambitions to vault by touring Yorkshire. The wisdom of so young a team marching into the very hotbed of rugby football, was much questioned the time but the Maritime struck out boldly, and returned with three out of four matches to their credit. The one they lost was at Wakefield Trinity, who had playing for them Freddy Lovett, whose splendid goal kicking really won the game. The visitors, however scored three tries. Two of them, Sam Vickers "pulled off", and in one of the instances he traversed half the length of the field. The club has established its reputation in Yorkshire. Dickenson, Sullivan, Williams, Vickers,

Murray, Stead and Devereaux, have from the first been the most promising players in the team. The record for 1891-91 was as follows: thirty six played, twenty four won, seven lost and five drawn. Total points for: two hundred and eighty, against: sixty eight. Stephen Sullivan now captains the amalgamated team, Tudor Foster plays for Llwynypia, whilst Willie Parkin has been supplanted by Ivor Howells, the old member of the Pontypridd team.

The Trial Match

On September 9th 1892, the Pontypridd Football and Athletic Club held a trial match at Taff Vale Park before the selection of a team to play Newport Harriers in the opening match of the season. There were a large number of spectators present on this Saturday afternoon to watch a probable team play a possible team. The game was set rolling by Mr David Leyshon, the chairman of the local board and the first president of the new club, and was followed by a hearty burst of cheering. Much fine play was witnessed, the probable team winning by two goals and one try, to one goal and one try (13-8). The two teams were as follows:

Probables

Back, Alun Morgan; Threequarters, Sam Vickers, Ben Dickenson, Jack Murray, A B Evans; Halves, Harry Williams, Steve Sullivan (C); Forwards, Jack Hope, Tom Hemsworth, Jimmy Connelly, O Bowers, Tom Murray, Harry Stead, Ivor Howells, Patsy Devereaux.

Possibles

Back, Walter Gay; Threequarters, Benny Lewis, Jimmy Green, Rueben Richards, George Harry; Halves, Jimmy Lewis, Christmas Jones; Forwards, Willie Parkin, Bill John, Walter Davies, H Davies, Jack Wilkins, Seaton, Phil Jones, D Hunt, J Nicholas, Spencer.

When the team was announced for the opening game, it was noticeable that most of the old players were selected and Maritime men, on merit, a predominance, such men as Tom Murray and Jimmy Connelly, who had both played in a Welsh trial the previous season, and Stead, Hemsworth, Green and Dickenson, could hardly be equalled. The halves were Messrs Stephen Sullivan and Harry Williams, the best in the district. The full team selected was:

Back, Alun Morgan; Threequarters, Jack Murray, Jimmy Green, Ben Dickenson, Sam Vickers; Halves, Stephen Sullivan (C), Harry Williams; Forwards, Jimmy Connelly, Tom Hemsworth, Harry Stead, Patsy Devereaux, Ivor Howells, O Bowers, Tom Murray, Jack Hope.

Pontypridd Amalgamated Football and Athletic Club
1892-93

Ben Lewis, Alun Morgan, Tom Murray
Jack Murray, Patsy Devereaux, Tom Hemsworth, A B Evans
Jack Wilkins, William Gay, Harry Wiliams, Ack Llewellin, Harry Stead, Willie Parkins, Tom Bryant
Jimmy Green, Jimmy Lewis

Mr David Leyshon
First President Of The Amalgamated Club

Mr David Leyshon was owner of the Newbridge Brewery, local councillor and a member of the local board of health. He was involved with the Maritime Colliery team until it merged with the Pontypridd club and became the first chairman of the club that initially was called 'The Pontypridd Football and Athletic Club'.

'Vericus' in the Pontypridd Chronicle commented:

'Although the majority of the team are "Maritime" men, its constitution is all that could be desired. Of course the committee cannot please everyone and as there are grumbles to be found in every community, so there are in Pontypridd, but I hardly believe this team could be improved upon. It seems a pity a place has not been reserved for Ben Tiley, the old favourite, but the probable cause can be found in the rumour that is circulating that Tiley is preparing a team of his own. Be that as it may, Tiley, although probably a good player, would hardly be able to play and please the present team, for, to say the least, he generally plays a selfish game. He does not understand combination play, whereas the newly formed club is nothing if not unselfish. At any rate, it is generally understood that Tiley will not play for Pontypridd this season.

The Season Begins

On September 17th 1892, the Pontypridd Rugby Football Club's history entered a new chapter when the "Pontypridd Football and Athletic Club" ran out for its first fixture in their new black and white jerseys for a home fixture against Newport Harriers. The towns football followers, who had awaited this match with such eagerness, found the wait well worth while because their club emerged with a resounding victory. The chief feature of the match was the magnificent passing of the home team and this was put down to the proper training of the Pontypridd captain, Stephen Sullivan, who had undoubtedly studied the game, and having come to the conclusion that in the long run it was far better to play an unselfish game, had taught his men accordingly. Six goals and four tries to nil (38-0) was a score to be proud of, especially when it was considered that their opponents were by no means a poor team.

Llwynypia "Fagged Out"

There was rejoicing in Pontypridd on September 24th 1892, when it became known that the town club, who were unchanged from the initial match, had not only defeated Llwynypia on their own ground, but had won by two goals and three tries to nil (19-0) and had prevented the homesters from scoring. The visitors had acted in concert from beginning to end, and their superior strength told, while Llwynypia were "fagged out" before the first half was over. Jimmy Green, the Pontypridd centre, showed good form and scored three tries, but, added one local newspaper *"his kicking was not up to scratch!"* Tudor Foster, the ex-Maritime centre, appeared for Llwynypia, and was, with all due respect to the referee, offside more than half his time. For the greater part of the second half Pontypridd were scoring tries in amazing rapidity.

Ungrateful Club

The new club had made a good start, but with all the changes throughout the summer, the fact that the club had changed its headquarters from the Sportsman Hotel to the Victoria Hotel had gone unreported. But that fact had made some people unhappy. This letter appeared in the "Free Press" on September 24th 1892:

'Dear Sir - Being an old footballer, I would like to know why the Pontypridd Football Club has left their headquarters at the Sportsman Hotel. Was the place too comfortable for them? Was there too much kindness bestowed upon their ungrateful heads? What man did more for the club than the late Mr Parry-Thomas? To forget his widow and little ones now is anything but brave and noble, two qualities supposed to be taught by the British outdoor sports. Will anyone explain?

Yours Truly "Footballer"

There was no reply from the club but, perhaps the promise of a room being altered into a gymnasium at the Victoria Hotel had persuaded them to move from the Sportsman Hotel.

A Stern Test

Pontypridd were unchanged for the third consecutive match when Cardiff Harlequins, who were considered the first stern test for Pontypridd, and who had beaten both Pontypridd and Maritime last season, visited Taff Vale Park on October 1st 1892. The game was fast and vigorous but despite exerting a lot of first half pressure, Pontypridd were trailing at halftime to a penalty goal. As the second half progressed the spectators became extremely boisterous, and this increased when Jimmy Green just failed to score. Play continued to be very exciting, the spectators rushing up and down the field following play. The homesters made frequent attempts to get over and when the excitement was at its highest, Jimmy Green picked up and scored a try amidst tumultuous cheering. Ben Dickensons kick was a failure, but a famous result for Pontypridd had been secured, and the local spectators who had witnessed this draw were of the opinion that the new club would do them proud this season. Final score: Pontypridd one try, Cardiff Harlequins one penalty goal (3-3).

Strike Fears

A week later, October 8th 1892, Llandaff, who were extensively billed as the South Wales Cupholders, were the visitors to Taff Vale Park. It was feared that a strike at the Maritime colliery would play havoc with the constitution of the home club, of which no fewer than nine or ten players were employed there. It was gratifying to learn that most of the men had found work at the Great Western Colliery adjoining. A fairly large crowd, but not nearly as large as the week before, saw a somewhat disappointing game, and the score, Pontypridd three tries, Llandaff one try (9-3), should have been different.

The play of the homesters was not as neat as expected, but on the form shown they should have crossed the Llandaff line at least half-a-dozen times but when they were within an ace of scoring, a slovenly pass, or a mull of some kind or another, interfered and prevented them accomplishing their desire. The home pack played a rattling good game, Jimmy Connelly and Tom Hemsworth being the most brilliant. At threequarter, the "bun" went to Jimmy Green, whose play was not marred by a single mistake. One victory for Llandaff though, was that they became the first visitors to score a try at

Taff Vale Park. 'Toricus' in a local newspaper commented:

'The time advertised for kick-off was 4.15, but they actually kicked off forty five minutes after this. Considering the early hour at which darkness descends, 4.15 is in all conscience late enough for a start, but at 5 o'clock it is really time to wonder if it is worth starting at all. Looking at the hundreds of spectators who risked rheumatic and every other kind of "atic" hanging around for the start, it was seen that directly that halftime sounded, darkness came on apace, rendering it almost impossible for the spectators lining the ropes to distinguish individual play. It is hoped that those in charge will see to it that games commence earlier, for there is no excuse for keeping spectators waiting for threequarters of an hour.'

An Exciting Draw

Pontypridd visited Aberavon on October 15th 1892 and played a no score draw in what was described as a brilliant and scientific match. The first half, though exciting, had ended scoreless, but in the second half for a while Pontypridd seemed to have it all their own way, but in the scrums the superior brutal strength of the Avonites told. Later, the homesters resorted to passing, but made a very poor show, the tackling of the visitors being too sure. Towards the end, Ben Lewis attempted a penalty goal for Pontypridd, but trusting too much, the wind sent the ball wide of the posts. Again the Avonites looked like scoring, but bit by bit, however, the danger was overcome and Pontypridd were once more invading the home ground when the final whistle blew.

Cardiff's Narrow Victory

For some weeks before October 20th 1892, Pontypridd's home match with Cardiff had been the sole topic of discussion amongst local football enthusiasts, and this enthusiasm had not been confined to just Pontypridd either, as the prospect of this match had been the subject of general inquiry throughout the football world. The previous Pontypridd results had placed them on top of the tree as "foremen worthy of their steel" through the country. In view of these circumstances the home supporters had every hope of their representatives giving a good account of themselves. It was in the recollection that Pontypridd were defeated in their initial match in Cardiff last season, but retrieved their loss later in the season by defeating them by a narrow margin. This was a huge success, and judging by the players that the Cardiff Committee had sent up this time, they had recognised the fact that Pontypridd were now a team of established merit, and worthy of giving them a good game.

The home team had been in training every night that week and had availed themselves of the People's Park, Mill Street, where they could be seen racing around the enclosure. The team selected was the same as that which had played Cardiff Harlequins and Aberavon recently, with one exception, Harry Williams's place at half being taken by Tudor Foster, formerly a Maritime player, but now playing for Penygraig. As time drew near for the kick-off, hundreds of spectators wended their way to the Taff Vale grounds. There was a large influx of visitors from Cardiff, the Taff Vale Railway company running up a special train. The enclosure was crowded with spectators, the grandstand being packed. The Pontypridd committee had wisely looked ahead and had the "field of battle" in good condition, and arrangements were everything that could be desired. As the teams entered the arena they were given a hearty reception by their supporters.

Lewis kicked off for Cardiff, and Sullivan, the home captain, obtained and kept the ball selfishly, a few yards only being gained. Some equal and tight scrums now became frequent. The next bit of conspicuous play was Norman Biggs skipping down into home territory, but his attempt to score was frustrated by Jimmy Green, who collared for Pontypridd in excellent style. The visitors pressed for a time and from a line-out near the grandstand, a short run was made for the home line, and from a clever reversal from an ensuing scrum, Elliott passed to Biggs, but henceforth the ball was lost. Tudor Foster afterwards removed play towards the Cardiff line. Strenuous efforts were made by both sides to score, and eventually the ball emerged from a scrum on the Cardiff side, and Sweet Escott gave to Fustian, who after gaining round passed to Biggs, who in turn passed to Elliott, the latter scoring. The attempt at goal was a failure. After the restart Sam Vickers distinguished himself for the homesters with a short but brilliant run. After the ball returned to the centre, a rush down the field by Pontypridd was deservedly cheered. This was soon after repeated in good style, and Pontypridd secured a minor. Stephen Sullivan soon after put in a strong kick towards the visitors line, Ivor Howells all but scoring. The home boys were now working splendidly and made play exceedingly exciting. Just before halftime, Jimmy Connelly picked up from a scrum and nearly got over.

A short interval for refreshments was taken, the prospects of the final result being widely discussed by the spectators. Jack Hope kicked off for Pontypridd. Play soon moved to the home 25, where a tight scrum was formed and Harry Stead, a home forward, started a clever rush to the centre, and the home forwards backing up well, forced the play, but Biggs relieved with a gigantic kick. Later, play was now confined to the visitors 25, but Pontypridd never got near enough to become dangerous. Mulling by the Cardiff backs brought excretion from their supporters. At this time too, the referee had to interview and caution certain players for roughness. Proceeding to play vigorously, both teams gave the spectators an excellent exhibition of the game of football. During some scrambled play Elliott was seen making for the home line, but there was not a single Cardiff back on hand to follow him and take his pass, so the oval was rushed into touch, nothing further occurring until the final whistle. The Pontypridd team that day was: Back, Alun Morgan; Threequarters, Jack Murray, Jimmy Green, Ben Dickenson, Sam Vickers; Halves, Stephen Sullivan (C), Tudor Foster; Forwards, Jimmy Connelly, Tom Hemsworth, Tom Murray, Harry Stead, J O Bowers, Patsy Devereaux, Ivor Howells, Jack Hope.

Charity Match Failure

Pontypridd's brave defeat by Cardiff was followed a week later by a one goal to nil (5-0) victory in Morriston.

The ground was in a wretched condition, but A B Evans scored the only try after running from halfway and eluded the home fullback for a fine try.

The strike at the Maritime colliery was apparently still continuing, and on November 3rd 1892, the Pontypridd Football Club had arranged a charity game to benefit the sufferers of the stoppage, when a Rhondda District team visited Taff Vale Park. The match, however, was not a financial success. A local newspaper commented:

> *'Perhaps the Rhondda side was not of sufficient class to command a good gate, but still, the "generous" public of which we hear so much, could have come out in a little better style than it did.'*

The same day the Western Mail published the current playing records of the leading Welsh clubs:

	p	w	d	l	f	a
Cardiff	8	5	3	0	65	36
Swansea	7	4	2	1	52	39
Penarth	8	4	4	0	48	65
Newport	6	6	0	0	123	3
Cardiff Qns	7	4	2	1	58	19
Llanelly	7	1	5	1	15	59
Aberavon	8	3	3	2	24	32
Penygraig	9	3	1	5	50	25
Pontypridd	8	4	1	3	72	14
Neath	8	4	1	3	36	24
Morriston	8	4	2	2	47	14

Ponty Make Draw With 'Kyites

On November 5th 1892, Pontypridd drew at home with Treorchy by one try each (3-3). 'Marcaman' in the Pontypridd Chronicle told how the home side were over confident of victory:

'Ponty had a "big thing" going on when they met Treorchy. This being so, it was only to be expected that they would again prove how ludicrous they can be at times, for lo and behold, they succeeded in making a draw with the "'Kyites". Pontypridd are really so fond of misunderstanding their opponents that their spectators are just beginning to get quite used to the "spasmodic" form which they have shown this season.

For this, Pontypridd have no-one to blame but themselves. Whenever they think they have a "soft thing" on, there is no attempt at training, and they do not believe in keeping themselves in even ordinary form. The result is that they are caught napping. It is a remarkable circumstance that while Pontypridd generally make a capital showing against teams of superior calibre, they are rarely able to hold their own against what they consider to be inferior clubs. This has again been the case this season, for so far, the town team has not achieved a single win of note.'

Hull Britannia Defeated

After being fairly sat upon by Cardiff Harlequins two days before, Hull Britannia came on to Pontypridd on November 7th 1892, to meet an unrepresentative lot of the "black and white" brigade. The game was not a very interesting one and it was plain from the outset that whoever won, it would only be by the skin of their teeth, and so it proved, for the homesters just managed to win by one try to nil (3-0). All through the game, not a little science was displayed by either side, and although at the start things were made a little lively, afterwards it degenerated into a mere scramble. However, scramble or no scramble, it would be idle to deny that the homesters were exceptionally lucky in winning, for by far the greater portion of the game was contested in the home territory. Time after time did the visitors get within an ace of scoring, and had they possessed just a little more combination, they might have scored on several occasions. As it was, they were defeated by a try by A B Evans.

The same day as the Hull Britannia match, Pontypridd players, Jimmy Green, Harry Stead, Alun Morgan and Ivor Howells were appearing somewhere in a Welsh trial match.

Where's The Pontypridd Captain?

For a few matches there had been no reference to Pontypridd captain, Stephen Sullivan and it appears that he might have moved out of the district, but no explanation appears to have been published. We must assume that vice-captain, Alun Morgan would take over, but being a bit of a character who often had "run ins" with the club committee, he appears not to have lasted long. It was not until December that a local newspaper reported that Ack Llewellin, who had retired at the end of last season after being captain for the previous two years, would once more return to the helm as club captain.

No Disgrace

Pontypridd in all its previous encounters with Llanelly, had never been successful in gaining a win, but in all phases of this home game on November 12th 1892, they gave them a really good match. This time, after a stubborn fight, they were compelled to go under, the visitors just managing to plant themselves home by a drop goal to nil (4-0), which was a lucky score; for the goal they kicked by Harry Rees, which was brought off just before halftime, was more lucky than anything previously seen this season.

That the sides were evenly matched is self evident by the result, but Pontypridd ought to have won - and would have done had they been favoured by half the luck of the visitors - was also evident. For time after time they were within an ace of scoring, only to be prevented by sheer bad luck. However, to succumb to Llanelly is no disgrace and the narrow victory was nothing for Llanelly to make a song and dance about, particularly when it was remembered that Pontypridd had "deucedly" bad luck. The Pontypridd team versus Llanelly was:

Back, Walter Gay; Threequarters, Alun Morgan, A B Evans, Ben Dickenson, Jack Murray; Halves, H Williams, Jimmy Green; Forwards, Harry Stead, Ivor Howells, Tom Hemsworth, Patsy Devereaux, Jack Hope, Jack Wilkins, Jimmy Connelly, O Bowers.

A reporter in the Llanelly Guardian commented:

'I did not care much about going to Pontypridd. In the first place the weather was not very inviting and secondly, Pontypridd is, to say the least of it, anything but an inviting spot. The whole of the Rhondda valley for that matter, is much the same. It is said of a certain place that "prospects pleases and only man is vile". In the

Rhondda valley, however, although man is decidedly vile, every prospect does NOT please. I wished to report on the Swansea v Newport match, but my editor send me to Pontypridd whether I liked it or not.

The railway company, with their usual courtesy, did not provide us with a saloon and as a consequence the team was spread out over sundry compartments. If you have travelled by train to Pontypridd, you know you must change in Neath, and on that station we met the Newport XV travelling to Swansea. Later, as we travelled up the Neath valley, the sky rapidly became murky, until the clouds blotted the sun from the sky. The next halt was at Quakers Yard, where we had a half hour wait. This was taken advantage of as the captain distributed sandwiches and steaming hot cups of Bovril, refreshing us after our long journey, and we arrived in Pontypridd shortly before two o'clock.

For the match, I sat in the stand with the local reporter "Old Stager", who being a betting man backed Pontypridd with a 10/- bet. I told him to be prepared to pay up, and as soon as the two teams entered the arena, he tumbled to the fact that Llanelly were fitter and were bound to outstay their opponents. The Taff Vale ground is awkwardly situated. The River Taff runs alongside and a fairly strong kick often sends the leather right into the middle of the stream. This happened several times, the offenders being the Llanellyites, who were continually forgetting that the river ran in such close proximity. The match was exciting, and Llanelly were the better team from beginning to end, the ball being in the homesters 25 for fully fifty minutes, and should have scored two or *three tries to nil, rather than one drop goal to nil. After the match, the team took tea at the County Restaurant, Mill Street, and I was joined by "Old Stager" who paid up, and expressed the opinion that the visitors should have won by much more, and that the homesters compared to Llanelly looked "flabby" and "beefy".*

Unfortunate Incident At Neath

Neath were minus five of their regular players when they entertained Pontypridd on November 19th 1892. The visitors went down determined to do all that they knew to win, and play was decidedly in their favour in the first half, and at the interval the Neath partisans were freely discussing the disadvantages of being short of so many regulars. In the second half Pontypridd immediately pressed, and, after some pretty play Harry Williams got over with a try, but Alun Morgan failed with the kick. Some neat passing by Steer and Trick gained ground for the homesters. Relief was brought, but without any loss of time Neath again exhibited dash and Cross Got over and Lloyd Morgan converted. Neath again played with vigour, and again looked like scoring, and Pontypridd were hemmed into their own quarters until the end, leaving the homesters victors by one goal to one try (5-3). One incident, shortly before the end, clearly upset the Western Mail correspondent, who wrote:

'The charging down of Trick by Tom Hemsworth was a most unfortunate incident. Trick was seriously injured. Hemsworth displayed a great lack of judgement in charging in so furiously, as the ball had been kicked by Trick some seconds before he was run into. An

allowance should be made for the unavoidable excitement produced by the game, but at the same time it is proper to add that a heavier player should exercise some approach to discretion in running at a player much lighter than himself.'

Welsh Trial At Taff Vale Park

On December 3rd 1892, Pontypridd had the honour to receive players from different teams to engage in a trial match to select players to take part in the international matches for that season. The event of this important match being played at Pontypridd stamped the town as fully recognised football town. In the annals of football, the match would always be remembered as one of decided merit, and therein Pontypridd football enthusiasts were given an exhibition of the noble game like they had never witnessed before. Special trains were run from almost every important town in the principality and consequently a large number of supporters of each player entered the town. Quite an exodus of visitors came in by the two o'clock trains and the principal streets were almost blocked. As the time grew near from the commencement of the game, large crowds could be seen wending their way to the scene of battle, the Taff Vale Park.

Two teams were selected to decide between for international honours, and were named "Possibles" and "Probables". The "Probables" were a team selected by the Welsh Football Union committee as the most likely team to represent Wales; and the "Possibles" were selected by the same committee as worthy players upon which the committee could rely upon in case of absentees. It was seen that two local lads, Tom Hemsworth and Harry Stead, were selected to play for the "Possibles", a fact that did the town great credit. The ground was very sloppy and consequently accurate play was almost out of the question. Every part of the field was taken up by an eager crowd of spectators, and the banks and railway around the field were thronged by enthusiastic crowds, who saw the "Probables" emerge victors by one goal and three tries to one goal (14-5).

The Western mail reported:

'The attendance was a capital one, £56 being taken on the gate. Considering this match was played on a new and not very convenient to get to ground like Pontypridd, this must be regarded as very encouraging and should induce the Welsh Union to bring off all Trial matches at the grounds of rising or struggling clubs. The game cannot fail to have got a lift in the Pontypridd district owing to this fixture.'

The two teams that played in this Trial match were:

Probables: Back, W J Bancroft (Swansea);
Threequarters, A J Gould (Newport), Pearson and Norman Biggs (both Cardiff), A N Other; Halves, H P Phillips (Newport), Wat Thomas (Neath); Forwards, A F Hill (Cardiff), A W Boucher, J Hannen, W H Watts, T Day (all Newport), F Hutchinson (Neath), S Rice (Swansea), W Phillips (Cardiff Harlequins).

Possibles: Back, T England (Newport); Threequarters, P M Garret (Penarth), E Thorogood (Swansea), C Wilding

(Cardiff Harlequins), C S Coke (Swansea); Halves, R B Escott (Cardiff), Ivor Grey (Morriston); Forwards, T Jones, A Lewis (both Cardiff), Harry Stead (Pontypridd), H J Daniels (Llanelly), W Cope (Cardiff), H A Harris (Aberavon), Tom Hemsworth (Pontypridd).

Match Abandoned

The first half of Pontypridd's home match against St Davids on December 5th 1892, was scoreless, and the second was played in a blinding snowstorm. Several times Pontypridd had attacked the home citadel most fiercely and loud shouts went forth, the spectators being under the impression that Pontypridd had crossed the line. Eventually, Sam Vickers picked up and made a fine sprint to score in the left corner. Because of the snowstorm blowing diagonally across the field, the place kick was a failure. It was now impossible to distinguish or identify the players, and it was thought ten minutes after the resumption of play that the contestants should abandon the match with the homesters leading by one try to nil (3-0).

We Conquered

"We came, we saw, we conquered!" acclaimed the Pontypridd spectators after their pets had waged war against the Rhondda champions at Penygraig on December 19th 1892. The game was by no means a brilliant exposition, and indeed the greater portion of the latter half was contested in semi-darkness. Up to halftime, honours were even, nothing definite having been scored, in fact the latter half was far spent when a wild yell of delight broke from the handful of "Black and

White" supporters, signalling the fact that something substantial had been done, and then it was learned, for it was much too dark to be able to distinguish for oneself, that O Bowers had scored for the visitors. This was the only tangible score and Pontypridd retired the victors by one try to nil (3-0).

The Western Mail reported:

'The try by which Penygraig were beaten was notched in the latter part of the game, when it was impossible to distinguish the contest from the other side of the field. It was scored in extra-ordinary circumstances. One of the visitors, followed closely by Ben Phillips, leaped over the leather over the Penygraig line, but neither touched it. Bowers, who was racing up behind, fell upon the ball and loud shouts went forth proclaiming the glad tidings to the visiting friends around the ropes. It was stated by Penygraig that the try should not have been allowed. It was evident that Phillips would have been able to prevent the score had he been able to pull up as he crossed the line, but the ground was so hard and slippery after the morning frost, that he passed by the ball. The game at this point was rapidly growing to a close and the majority of spectators had made up their minds as the result, and had left before the last incident, and there must have been much discussion in the local taverns afterwards.'

Ack Takes Over

The Western Mail of December 16th 1892, carried this item with no explanation of what had happened to Steve Sullivan the Pontypridd captain: *"At a meeting of the*

Pontypridd Football Club, Mr Ack Llewellin was unanimously elected captain of the premier team, and Mr Ben Lewis, skipper of the second team."

The Christmas Tour

On Christmas Eve 1892, Pontypridd began a tour of Yorkshire with a match against Wortley, where they secured a three goals and three tries to nil (24-0) victory. On Boxing Day they met Sowerby Bridge on a hard ground, even though it had been covered by several inches of straw previous to the match being played. Pontypridd emerged victors from this game by four tries to one (12-3). The following day they played Hull Britannia before over 2,000 spectators, Ben Tiley securing a draw (3-3) with a try near the posts. Pontypridd's last match, at Hunslet on December 28th, was postponed due to a waterlogged field.

No Game

Following their return to Wales and the Wales v England match on January 7th 1893, South Wales suffered a snow fall, but on the following Saturday a fair contingent of Pontypridd supporters accompanied the team to the fixture at Cardiff Harlequins, but were disappointed to find the game postponed because a fair fall of snow still covered the field.

Brilliant Defence

There was a fair crowd present for Pontypridd's visit to Llanelly on January 21st 1893. The visitors were minus Ben Dickenson, Sam Vickers and Ben Tiley from the back division; and Jack Hope from the forwards.

Although the team might have suffered as a consequence, it cannot be denied that excellent substitutes were found. Forward, Jimmy Connelly, played fullback. The game was an exciting one, a number of incidents occurring to arouse the spectators. The homesters certainly held the reins in the aggressive part of the game, and it was surprising that they did not add several more tries to the two they secured. The absence of more scoring was principally due to the brilliant defence of the visitors, who tackled well and stopped the runs and rushes in a manner that commended itself to all. Indeed, their admirable defence was the feature of the match and had it not been so stubbornly consistent, the score of two tries to nil (6-0) would have been much greater. The Pontypridd team for this game was:

Back, Jimmy Connelly; Threequarters, Jimmy Green, Alun Morgan, Ben Lewis, Jack Murray; Halves, Harry Williams, Jimmy Lewis; Forwards, Harry Stead, Tom Hemsworth, Tom Murray, Patsy Devereaux, Ack Llewellin (C), Jack Wilkins, Tom Bryant, Willie Parkins.

Penygraig's Poor Show

Penygraig were said to have made a very poor show in their third meeting of the season with Pontypridd, at Taff Vale Park on February 6th 1893. Both had long been contesting the unofficial championship of the Rhondda and anyone who knew anything about football in the hills remembered the stubborn match last season, which it was agreed would decide the championship once and for all, that unhappily ended in a draw. But after the experiences of this season, few will deny that it has been fairly won by Pontypridd. Out of the three matches played, the first ended as a draw, and the other two ended in decisive victories for Pontypridd.

In this match, the Rhondda premier side suffered at the hands of the amalgamated club, a defeat the like of which they had never before experienced. They were fairly outclassed, and their supporters sought to minimise the defeat by pointing to the number of their absentees, but their substitutes were men of tried ability from the best teams in the Rhondda. The wonder is that Pontypridd did not pile on the score, for once the leather was secured by their backs, it was simply a case of rushing through the visiting forwards, only, however, to have to cope with the stubborn defence of Lloyd, the visiting custodian. The homesters, one and all, played beautifully. Seldom had the forwards been seen to better advantage, Harry Stead shining in the loose, while Tom Murray did heaps in the scrummage. The halfbacks played a good game, but should have passed more frequently. Jimmy Green had very little to do at threequarter, but what he had to do he did well. Walter Gay seemed to be gaining of late but seemed to lose his head when confronted by one or two opponents.

The only scored of the first half was a try by Jimmy Lewis, who scored within two minutes of the start, amidst great applause. The Penygraig men claimed a foul because the corner flag was knocked down, but the referee allowed it. Midway through the second half, Harry Williams obtained and transferred to Ben Lewis. The latter, on being collared, threw to Tom Hemsworth, who planted the oval behind the posts, amidst more great applause. Harry Williams's kick at goal was charged down. The homesters from here until the call of time kept their opponents penned in to run out winners by two tries to nil(6-0).

Unexpected Defeat For Neath

Neath suffered an unexpected defeat by two tries to nil (6-0) in Pontypridd on February 11th 1893 but all that saw the game agreed that the best team had won. The game though, all through was not far removed from a scramble, while good scientific play was entirely out of the question in the second half due to the drenching showers of rain. But even in the first half the Neath men had considerably the worse of the play, and although Pontypridd did not gain their first try until a few minutes before the interval, the ball was almost entirely confined to the visitors 25. The match was very disappointing from a spectators point of view. Only one bout of passing did the visitors succeed in bringing about and not once in the game did the Neathites look dangerous and only once reached the home 25 flag, but were penned in their own 25 for two thirds of the game. The home forwards played a hard game, especially in the second half considering that they had the wind and the rain in their faces. Harry Stead never played a better game than he did in this match. It was a treat to witness the way in which he broke through the scrums and was undoubtedly the best forward on the field. He was closely followed by the other Pontypridd forward, Tom Hemsworth. According to paper form, the Neath halfbacks were head and shoulders above Harry Williams and Jimmy Lewis, but they were simply not in it. The Pontypridd halves deserve praise for the clever manner in which they parted with the ball. The only score of the first half came just before lemons. Harry Williams beat Thomas and passed to Ben Tiley, who threw to Alun Morgan. He, on being collared, transferred to Jimmy Lewis, who eluded the fullback to score in the corner. The second try was scored mid-way through the second half. Harry Stead, Tom Murray and Jack Wilkins, broke through the Neath defence with a rush. Stead picked up, passed to Murray, who threw to Wilkins, which enabled the latter to score. Harry Williams again failed to convert. The Pontypridd team versus Neath was:

Back, Walter Gay; Threequarters, Ben Tiley, Alun Morgan, Jack Murray, Ben Lewis; Halves, Harry Williams and Jimmy Lewis; Forwards, Ack Llewellin (C), Harry Stead, Tom Murray, Tom Hemsworth, Jack Wilkins, Patsy Devereaux, Willie Parkin, Tom Bryant.

A Curious Report

The Pontypridd Chronicle of February 18th 1893, carried this curious report about the supposed life of a rugby football:

Trials Of A Football

Dedicated to the Pontypridd Football Club

I am only a piece of leather containing an inflated bladder - a harmless enough thing in my way, but the manner in which I am pummelled and badgered is sickening. All through this blessed football season I have every Saturday been taken from the hut on the Taff Vale

Grounds and kicked by one, cuffed by another, and half suffocated in the presence of hundreds of spectators, who seem to have no compassion or humanity in them, but cheer and applaud any of the cruel fellows who kick me the hardest or hold on to me the tightest. Only last Saturday as ever was, a lot of young sparks came up from Neath to cruelly ill treat me, as if it was not enough for the fifteen men who compose what they call the Pontypridd Football team, to be knocking me about all week. The heartless bipeds ranged themselves one lot on one side of the field and the other lot on the other side. Then that cruel fellow Ack Llewellin gave me a kick right on my tender end, and sent me flying over the heads of the men facing him. A cowardly individual from Neath kicked me back, and I was seized by about half-a-dozen fellows, who rudely fell upon me, nearly bringing my dinner up. A little gentleman called the "referee", seeing that I was not having fair play, blew a whistle and allowed me to draw a little air. But I did not remain unmolested for long, for I was thrown in among sixteen or seventeen of them, and then kicked this way and that until I had hardly any breath in my body. I was sent scudding along the field and Ben Tiley tried to catch me, but I eluded his grasp and heard him say "D--------" quite distinctly. After being badgered for about quarter of an hour I began to feel desperate and getting between Jack Nicholas's legs, tripped him over. As he fell I heard him mutter "blankety-blank-blank-blank". Suddenly A B Evans pounced upon me, but no sooner did he collar me than half-a-dozen fellows fell on him, and the air was full of "blanks". Will this never end? I said to myself as I went flying over towards Alun Morgan, who tried to seize me, but I bounded over his head. I will not be certain as to the character of the words used by Alun, but I believe I saw a patch of grass scorched up where he had been standing. The treatment I received during the next few minutes was horrible. My poor sides are aching now from the effects of it. When I got near Benny Lewis, he clutched me in a most ungentlemanly fashion, and used undue force in propelling me into mid-air. I descended among the Neath cannibals, who began to kick me up the field one after the other. Bill Williams tried to sit on me, but I turned over, and he sat upon a small stone, which also set him off "dynamiting". Bowers thought he would give me a powerful kick, but I just got out of the way in time, and the force of his kick caused the lace of his boot to snap. J E James, in the course of a scrimmage (I think that is what they term it), placed his face lovingly in mine, but I knew his caress was faithless and I withdrew my body, suddenly leaving his nose grating against a piece of bare ground. I am almost certain he said something which referred to the antipodes of Pontypridd, but I could not swear to it (although Ben Tiley probably would).

Davies and Clapp of Neath, then commenced peppering me with their hobnails, and sent me flying into the river. "At last I have escaped" I said, as I buried my aching head in the cooling waters, "Providence has turned against the inhuman brutes!" I thought, but I congratulated myself too soon, for a young barefooted ragamuffin (who I discovered afterwards was paid for the job) ran in after me and brought me out. They then commenced kicking me again, and did so with redoubled vigour, encouraged by the applause of Teddy Lewis, who after each attack on my poor body shouted out form the grandstand "Well kicked sir!" I wish Teddy had to take my place for only one Saturday afternoon. The referee blew his whistle, and I was once more taken to the kindly shelter of the hut, in order that my hurts might heal in time for next Saturday. Hood must have been thinking of the trials of a football when he wrote: *"Alas for the rarity of human charity amongst football teams"'*

Another Penygraig Fixture

The following fortnight Pontypridd had easy wins at Treorchy, by two tries to nil (6-0), a one try all home draw with Aberavon, and a seven tries to nil (21-0) home victory over Cogan. On March 3rd 1893, they travelled to Penygraig for the fourth meeting of the season, where the Belle Vue ground was in a very muddy condition, but the match proved to be very fast and exciting all the way through. But from a scientific point of view it was very disappointing, in as much as Penygraig did nothing but fall on the ball. This may be accounted for by the heavy condition of the ground and the greasiness of the ball, which rendered all passing of the ball impossible. If the ground had been in better condition, no doubt Pontypridd would have piled up a very big score, some of the minors being very narrow things for tries. The try that Tom Hemsworth scored, which was disallowed by the referee because it was a forward pass, should have been allowed because several spectators in line with the pass from Harry Stead stated that Hemsworth was about five yards behind. Pontypridd eventually emerged winners by one goal to nil (5-0), the only score coming mid-way through the second half. Jimmy Lewis obtained from a scrum, threw to Harry Williams, he to Jimmy Green, who after making three or four summersaults, scored a beautiful try, which Alun Morgan converted.

Cardiff Inflict A Heavy Defeat

Pontypridd up to this time had had a most successful time and their record read: Played 31, Won 21, Drawn 6 and Lost 4. The only defeats they had suffered were at the hands of Cardiff by a try to nil; to Neath by a goal to a try, and twice to Llanelly. But despite this they suffered a heavy nineteen point to nil defeat at Cardiff Arms Park on March 15th 1893. The Western Mail reported:

'With a strong wind behind their backs early on, the home forwards completley beat their lighter opponents and fed their backs in fine style, but as the game wore on, it was evident that despite this, they were not allowed to do what they liked. The Pontypridd eight consisted of eight hard working men, and with a little tuition would be hard to beat. Once the ball was in the open, however, the game was all in Cardiff's favour, the visiting backs being lacking in attack and unable to check the smart short passing. What Pontypridd lacked in attack they exhibited in stirling saving powers, pluckily fielding the ball in a manner that was characteristic of the whole team.'

The Glamorgan Free Press meanwhile, commented that Pontypridd did better than the final score indicated and wrote:

'Nobody thought for one moment that Pontypridd would win, but everyone expected the team to make a good attempt. The final score was no indication of the merits of the match, but if Pontypridd had had fair play, the score would have read: Cardiff two goals and two tries; Pontypridd one goal and two tries. The try that Jack Wilkins scored was in my opinion fair. The way in which he got over was this: The forwards took a dribble from the centre of the Cardiff 25, where Jack got over the line. E P Biggs mulled the ball and Wilkins fell on it, but it was disallowed. The try scored by Alun Morgan was similar to Biggs's try. Alun carried Biggs over the line as Biggs had carried Benny Lewis. Where Pontypridd lost it was in the quartet. The Cardiff four played a good game, their passing being executed with neatness and dispatch. Their forwards, however, were beaten but Pontypridd showed up well in the tight and loose. Tom Murray, Pontypridd, was the best forward on the field, closely followed by Devereaux, Stead and Wilkins. In fact, all the forwards played for all they were worth. Harry Williams was the best of the visiting halves, his passing and dribbling being excellent, and he and "Little Jar" completely smothered the home pair. Jimmy Green and Benny Lewis were the cream of the threequarters, whilst Jack Ewans played well as custodian, his kicks finding touch every time.

Pontypridd: Back, Jack Ewans; Threequarters, Ben Lewis, Alun Morgan, Jimmy Green, Jack Murray; Halves, Harry Williams + Jimmy Lewis; Forwards, Ack Llewellin (C), Harry Stead, Tom Hemsworth, Tom

Murray, Jack Wilkins, Patsy Devereaux, Willie Parkin, Tom Bryant.

A Fabulous Victory At St Helens

After a home win against Morriston on Saturday, March 18th, on Monday March 20th 1893, Pontypridd travelled for a first fixture against West Wales giants, Swansea. This match ought to have been played two days before on the Saturday but the field that day was being used for the Glamorgan v Lancashire match, in which Pontypridd forward, Harry Stead, had played. Included in the Pontypridd team were two unfamiliar names, Endascott and Oppoer, who had not been mentioned previously in the season. Were they Cardiff players brought in to play against Swansea? Harry Stead also played, his second match on St Helens in three days!

At 5.05 Pontypridd kicked of on a perfect ground. A minor was secured by the visitors soon after the start, and after the drop-out from the 25, play stayed in the home half, the visitors showing up well. Thereafter, Swansea got on the aggressive. A scrum was formed just opposite the Pontypridd goalposts, but Oppoer kicked the loose ball to mid-distance. Harry Stead and Patsy Devereaux then dribbled in good style and clean broke through the home defence, the visiting forwards rushing it over the line exacting a minor. After, Pontypridd had decidedly the better of matters for a few minutes and forced the game near the home 25. Gill Evans then transferred for Swansea to Whapham, who ran into the visitors half, where Endascott, the Pontypridd fullback, mulled the ball and allowed the home men a good chance of scoring. However, Jimmy Lewis got possession and ran well into the Swansea half. The homesters returned to the attack, but there was no major score before halftime.

After lemons, the home team kicked off, and at once acted on the aggressive. Harry Williams relieved for Pontypridd by putting in a well timed kick, but the homesters again attacked. Tom Murray changed play to neutral ground for a minute, but Gill Evans passed to Whapham, who got a corner try. W J Bancroft made a splendid attempt to kick a goal but failed. Swansea now led by a try to nil after a very hard game. Subsequently the home team forced their way into their opponents 25, and Jonah Morgan almost got over, the ball going into touch. After the throw in Harry Williams kicked well out of danger, and scrummages were formed in neutral territory. Harry Stead took the ball from Williams, who transferred to Jack Murray, but the last named lost the ball near the Swansea goal-line. A change now came over the scene, and Jimmy Green dropped a beautiful goal and Pontypridd now led by one point. Emboldened by this reversal, Swansea forged forward and worked the oval near the visitors goal-line and exacted a minor. Thereafter the game became very exciting, both teams playing with great energy. Endascott made his mark from a lofty kick, and Bancroft caught the ball and did the same, but nothing resulted. Oppoer failed to return, and Swansea were on the ball. A penalty kick was awarded to the homesters, and Bancroft sent the ball over the bar, but the referee disallowed the kick, it not being taken in the right position. Swansea now made strenuous efforts to score, and a scrum was formed close on the visitors goal-line, but by a capital rush and dribble, Pontypridd relieved in good style and carried the ball over the halfway line. Again, Swansea looked like scoring, but only secured a minor before time was called, leaving Pontypridd victors by one drop goal to one try (4-3).

The Daily Post, who normally gave good coverage for all Swansea games, gave a very small report on this match, but 'Vigilant' in the Pontypridd Herald wrote:

'The Swansea team was taken down by good old Ponty, and on their own ground too. In the first half Pontypridd penned them in their own 25, but with one or two exceptions, when Bancroft would put in a long kick, which would change the venue somewhat. So well did Pontypridd wheel the scrimmages that the home captain thought the Swansea pack only had seven men, and another was requisitioned, then it was seen that they had nine forwards, so he was sent back amidst much merriment. Well, it was a narrow victory, but one that Pontypridd ought to be proud of because taking down Swansea on their own ground is no mean task. The Pontypridd forwards played well. Tom Murray, Harry Stead and Tom Hemsworth were very prominent, their tackling being grand. Harry Williams and Jimmy Lewis were more than a match for the opposing halves, and put them entirely in the shade. The quartet played very well and preference was given to Jimmy Green and Alun Morgan. Green's drop goal was a beauty. Endascott was rather timid at fullback but on the whole did fairly well.'

The Pontypridd Chronicle of March 24th 1893 carried this report on the Swansea game:

Pontypridd Beat Swansea - A Glorious Victory

The Team Receives An Ovation

Great Enthusiasm at Pontypridd

'*When the Pontypridd football team journeyed to Swansea on the 4.40 train on Monday, all the members of the club thought of bringing off a good fight, but the idea that they would return victorious over the "Champions of the West" never crossed the brain of the most sanguine. However, it is the unexpected that happened, and before dusk a great surprise came over the Swansea people in the charge of a defeat upon their own ground by a team by which they had in the past considered much their inferior, and in fact a team too insignificant to give a fixture. Soon after the commencement of operations Pontypridd showed they meant business, and during the first half they had things all their own way. It was not until after the change of ends that Swansea had a look in, when they began to wake up a bit, but even then their passing was slovenly done. They obtained a solitary try but Jimmy Green - "Good old Greenie" as he is familiarly known - dropped a goal and won the match. The dash with which the Pontypriddians played proved that they were not a team to be ignored, and when the whistle blew they left the field having vanquished a team which is rarely defeated on its own ground.*'

Telegram after telegram arrived at Pontypridd conveying the welcome news of a glorious victory, and by eight o'clock all the town rang with the echoes of praise. A man who met another on the street broke out by asking:

> "Have you heard the news?"
> "What news?"
> "Why that Pontypridd beat Swansea today,
> a goal to a try!"
> "Hip Hip Hurrah!"

And the recipient of the news rushed up to Delaney's (a coffee house), to Frank Thomas's (my hatter), to the "Vic" (Victoria Hotel) and the White Hart Hotel, where the telegrams were exhibited. Great was the rejoicing, so great indeed, that hundreds of people went to the station to meet the eight o'clock train, under the impression that the team would return with it, but no, they were disappointed. The excitement in the town increased and everyone was talking of the famous victory. The enthusiastic public were anxious to give the team a right hearty welcome home, and Mr Teddy Lewis engaged the Pontypridd town band for the purpose of meeting them. Therefore, at half past eleven, a crowd numbering between 2,000 and 3,000 persons - men, women and children - with a larger number of torches - awaited the arrival of the team at the station, and just about the same time the Clarence Theatre poured out a few hundred more people to swell the crowd.

Just as the train steamed into the station the band struck "See the conquering heroes come" and Ack Llewellin, the clever and popular captain of the team, was literally dragged out of the compartment and immediately shouldered by his rejoicing admirers. The more enthusiastic of the crowd also shouldered Harry Stead and Jimmy Green. Then the vast concourse wended its way, headed by the band, through the streets of the town, which were lined with people and the cries of "Good only Ponty!" and "Good old Ack" were echoed far and near. Speeches were called for at the New Inn and here the enthusiasm of the crowd knew no bounds. The victorious captain was hoisted onto the wall from where he addressed the crowd, and in the course of a few remarks said that he felt particularly proud of his club that day (cheers). They had fought a stiff battle. Not only had they had to play against the Swansea team, but against the referee as well (loud applause). Last year they had beaten Cardiff and this year they beat Swansea, and he hoped that next season the team would be so efficient as to be able to beat Newport (loud cheers). Mr Harry Stead and Jimmy Green then addressed the crowd and were heartily applauded. The procession after this wended its way back again as far as the Victoria Hotel, the headquarters of the club, Llewellin, Stead and Green still being carried. When the "Vic" was reached further addresses were given by the captain and Teddy Lewis, the latter appealing for the public to support a team which had done so much for the honour of the town (cheers). So far, the team had not been recognised as it ought to be, but he sincerely hoped that in the future the public would rally around them and that the rich men of the town would put their hands in their pockets, and give all the encouragement they could to the Pontypridd Amalgamated Football Club (applause). The crowd having given to the team three hearty cheers, then dispersed.

First Class Now?

In the editorial of the same newspaper, this item appeared:

'The defeat of Swansea by the Pontypridd football team was altogether an unexpected event, but the news was generally welcomed. For years Swansea has posed as a first class team and the excuse they made that the team that played Pontypridd did not consist of their best team is bunkum. Pontypridd for years has been striving and persevering, and the game has been studied very carefully, yet, up to the present season they have hardly been recognised as first class team. Now at any rate they can claim that distinction. They have worked hard and fully deserve the honour that they have gained. Therefore we consider it a public duty to support the club. Not only by subscriptions, but also by gate money and the public of Pontypridd should take considerably more interest in the doings of the club. A word to the committee will not be out of place here. The end of the season is drawing nigh, but that ought not to be the reason why the club should rest during the summer. We are glad that amateur sports are contemplated, and we suggest the formation of a cycling club and other athletic clubs in connection with the Pontypridd amalgamated society during the summer.'

Determined Penarth

With the victory over Swansea still fresh in the Pontypridd supporters minds, most thought that the home side would defeat Penarth the following Saturday, March 25th 1893, and that the result was a foregone conclusion, and they were proved to be correct as to the result as Penarth were defeated by one drop goal and three tries, to one goal and one try (12-8) but not until after a stiff fight.

The match was fast and exciting, and the large concourse of spectators who assembled on the Taff Vale Park were amply rewarded. The visitors played in a most determined manner from start to finish. Their forwards worked hard in the tight and were very alert in the open, while their back division played splendidly, their passing, running and kicking were a treat to look at. For the homesters, at threequarter, Alun Morgan and A B Evans, were perhaps the pick. Morgan was now in splendid form, the way in which he, after a splendid round of passing, secured possession and dodged through the whole of the Penarth backs to score, was a veritable eye opener. Added to this a sensational drop goal from over half the length of the field, it must be admitted that he contributed more than his fair share towards securing victory. The third try of the match was got by A B Evans, and was the result of a splendid run from halfway, a performance that he nearly repeated later on. It is needless to say that each of these performances brought forth a hearty cheer from the crowd, who were evidently on the best of terms with themselves. The forwards, one and all played well, while Harry Williams and Jimmy Lewis at half, were too good for their opponents. The match throughout was indeed a splendid one, and this in conjunction with the glorious weather, made the matter almost perfect from the spectators point of view.

An Important Fixture

The previous season, Maritime had secured a 0-0 draw in Gloucester, and this must have led to this report that appeared in a local newspaper at the end of March 1893:

'I am given to understand that it is most probable that Pontypridd will pay a visit to Gloucester in a week or two. An offer has been made to the Pontypridd club by Gloucester to make the journey. Should the offer be accepted and I have every reason to believe it will, it is hoped that "our boys" will repeat the splendid performance at Swansea and return home victorious.'

However, this game, which would have been very prestigious game for Pontypridd, never came about.

Evans Knocks Llwynypia For Four

Pontypridd's match at Taff Vale Park on Monday, March 27th 1893, was played before a large number of spectators. Llwynypia won the toss and Pontypridd kicked off against the wind. Soon, the homesters made a rush and A B Evans kicked over the visitors line and drew first blood in the shape of a minor. Shortly after, he repeated the operation. After the drop-out Llwynypia rushed to the home 25, where A B Evans received from Alun Morgan and scored. The kick failed. The play then became very exciting, the visitors playing with real dash and pressed Pontypridd on their line until Harry Williams cleared. From a scrum, the same man got away and passed to A B Evans, who scored his second try. Alun Morgan again failed to convert. On resuming, the homesters continued to press and from a scrum Harry Williams threw again to Evans, who transferred to Morgan, who passed on to Rhys Davies, who scored an unconverted try. The visitors, nothing daunted, again played up with great spirit to the home quarter, but there were no further scores up to halftime.

Lemons over, the homesters with some splendid passing soon took play to the Llwynypia line, where Harry Williams procured and passed to A B Evans, who scored his third try. Alun Morgan this time converted to ironic cheers. On the recommencement the visitors obtained two minors in quick succession, Ben Phillips kicking over the line and Endascott touching down on both cases. On the restart the visitors again pressed, but grand passing enabled A B Evans, after eluding several opponents, to score his fourth try, this time between the posts, Alun Morgan converting. Shortly afterwards, Evans almost scored another, Llwynypia having to touch down. In the last minute Pontypridd exacted another minor, leaving them victors by two goals and four tries to nil (16-0).

A Disappointing Easter

After such a good run, Easter 1893 appears to have been a bit of a let down. Home games against Sowerby Bridge, on Good Friday, and Pontardawe the following day, went unreported and more than likely were postponed for some reason, perhaps the weather. And so it was on Easter Monday that Pontypridd ran out for their last arranged fixture of the season when they entertained Pontymoel.

Pontypridd, despite being without their skipper Ack Llewellin, and Tom Murray, Benny Lewis and A B Evans, ran out winners by one try to nil (3-0). The homesters kicked off and play settled down in the visitors 25. Pontymoel then broke away to the centre, but Jimmy Green dribbled back. The visitors with great dash again invaded the home 25, but Walter Gay saved. Pontypridd then played a combined game and rushed into the visitors 25, where Tom Hemsworth picked up and ran over for a try. Alun Morgan failed to convert. After the restart Rhys Davies made a good attempt to get over and forced a minor. Play was in the centre when halftime blew.

Early in the second moiety, Jimmy Green obtained and got away nicely. One of the visitors, coming at top speed, collided with Green very roughly, and Jimmy had to be carried from the field. Pontypridd, down to fourteen men, more than held their own, and some passing by their backs all but let Jack Murray score. Pontymoel then had to touch down in defence. From the drop-out, Alun Morgan got away but lost the ball on the line. After this the visitors rallied and penned the homesters in their own quarters, scoring three minors in succession. Shortly afterwards time was called.

Dr Howard Davies

Dr Howard Davies was the Chief Medical Officer for the local Board of Health, Medical Superintendent of the Smallpox Isolation Hospital and a member of the Education Committee of the Pontypridd Urban District Council. He was also medical officer to the Pontypridd Union, Workhouse, Infirmary and Cottage Homes; Recruiting Medical Officer for the Pontypridd District; Pontypridd Police Medical Officer and Medical Officer to the Maritime and Penrhiw Collieries.

It was Dr Davies who attended Noah Morgan at Taff Vale Park when the latter collapsed and died. He was also Vice-President with the Maritime Colliery team and instructed Jimmy Connelly on his diet as he tried to gain his Welsh cap. He also represented the colliery team in its talks with the Pontypridd club over the proposed amalgamation. On its completion, he took an automatic place on the new club committee and served the club for several years.

Great Western Colliery c1900

Disaster Strikes Local Colliery

Pontypridd Arrange Benefit Matches

Newport and Swansea XV's Visit The Town

So the 1892-93 season was over. But fate would decree that this was not so, for on April 11th 1893, tragedy struck the Pontypridd district when there was an explosion at the Great Western Colliery, Hopkinstown, which took the lives of fifty-eight men and boys. Immediately a disaster fund was set up and the Pontypridd Amalgamated Football Club, who had several men working at the colliery, set about arranging benefit matches for the funds set up for the families and dependants of those who had died. The whole of South Wales started fund-raising and the Cardiff and Newport clubs were asked to play in Pontypridd, but several players had gone on holiday as the season was over, and eventually they agreed to send a combined team to the town. Jack Bancroft, the Swansea captain, had also personally promised to bring up a team, but many regular Swansea men were unable to make the midweek fixture and eventually only four regulars made the trip, the rest of the team being made up of players from the Morriston club. The Glamorgan Free Press carried this report of the first benefit match against the Newport/Cardiff XV on April 21st 1893:

'The secretary of the Pontypridd club, Mr Edward Llewellin and the Athletic committee, with commendable promptitude acted upon the urgency of the case with a view to increasing the finds. In connection with others, Mr Llewellin had been busily engaged in

promoting the affair. The Newport team were asked to go on the matter, and, with characteristic generosity, fell in with the proposals and agreed to play a match wherein their principal players should take part. The event had been the topic of conversation amongst local football enthusiasts for the past week and the committee had worked assiduously and with untiring energy in pushing forward the sales of tickets, with the result that numerous quantities had been sold. In the selection of players, Newport had secured as good a team as possible considering the lateness of the season. Pontypridd in this respect availed themselves of the best talent that could be obtained.'

After five o'clock, the roads leading to Taff Vale Park were crowded with persons wending their way to the field of battle. The 4.30 trains had brought down quite and exodus of strangers from Newport, Cardiff and the Rhondda. The town itself presented a lively appearance, crowds assembling outside the Victoria Hotel, the headquarters of the Pontypridd club, and outside the New Inn Hotel, where the visitors put up. At about 5.15, almost every available space on the Taff Vale Park was occupied and every point of vantage taken up. The enclosure, grandstand etc were lined with crowds of eager spectators discussing the probabilities of the match. As the players entered the arena they were greeted with loud and continuous cheering. The Pontypridd team were the first to make their appearance, followed soon by the noted wearers of the Black and Amber. On the spin of a coin, fortune favoured the genial home captain, Ack Llewellin, who decided to kick-off from the town end.

Pontypridd kicked off against the wind, and the ball was returned to Alun Morgan, who then threw to Ben Tiley, who scored a try within a minute of the start. Alun Morgan failed to convert. Encouraged by this, the homesters kept the visitors penned in their own 25 for a considerable time. Norman Biggs at last changed the venue by a fine sprint to the centre, but Tom Hemsworth kicked back to his opponents 25, where England saved. Jones received for Newport, and after kicking down the line Alun Morgan touched down in defence. After the drop-out play settled down in the home 25, where a scrum was formed. Percy Phillips here obtained, and after a dodgy run scored a pretty try. Norman Biggs failed at goal. On resuming, some fine passing was witness from the home backs, which ended with Jimmy Green kicking in the Newport 25, where Pontypridd secured a minor. Just before halftime, Ben Tiley again got away to the visitors 25, where Jack Murray obtained on the wing and transferred to Tom Hemsworth, who scored. Alun Morgan failed to convert, leaving Pontypridd leaders at halftime by two tries to one.

After lemons, back and fore play ensued until Biggs made a sensational run to the home 25, where he was brought down by Jack Murray. After this the homesters made their way over halfway, but Phillips obtained and Biggs was again brought down, this time by A B Evans. Ben Tiley then broke away for Pontypridd, but Newport had a free, and fine passing by Gould and Biggs carried the hide to the line, where the latter got over, the same player having no difficulty in converting. On the restart the home forwards retaliated by making fine dribble to the 25, where some pretty passing was witnessed amongst the home backs. Ack Llewellin eventually picked up and threw to Jack Murray, who made a grand attempt at a drop goal, the ball striking one of the uprights and rebounded back into play. Pontypridd were later awarded a free from a mark, and Alun Morgan took the place for goal, but only a minor resulted. Time was called soon afterwards, leaving the visitors victorious by one goal and one try to two tries (8-6). The two teams that played that day were:

Pontypridd: Back, Alun Morgan; Threequarters, A B Evans, Jimmy Green, Ben Tiley, Jack Murray; Halves, Harry Williams and Jimmy Lewis; Forwards, Ack Llewellin (C), Harry Stead, Tom Hemsworth, Tom Murray, Patsy Devereaux, Jack Wilkins, Willie Parkin, Tom Bryant.

Newport/Cardiff XV: Back, Tom England;
Threequarters, A J Gould, G H Gould, Norman Biggs (Cardiff), J Elliott; Halves, H P Phillips, P C Parfitt; Forwards, T C Graham, T Pook, W Groves, J Rowley, T Newcombe and R Davies, S Cranon, Gus Lewis (all three Cardiff).

The Second Benefit Match

On April 28th 1893, Pontypridd played the second benefit match in aid of the Great Western Colliery disaster fund, when a Swansea/Morriston XV visited Taff Vale Park. the kick-off was arranged for 5pm, but the visitors missed their train connection in Cardiff, and when their scheduled train arrived in Pontypridd minus the team, hundreds of anxious spectators awaiting their arrival at the station were very disappointed. Fortunately, Jack Bancroft had wired the Pontypridd headquarters at the Victoria Hotel and asked if they should still come up. The Pontypridd club replied to the affirmative but it was not until 6.30 that the two sides entered the field of play, it having been decided to play only twenty minutes each way.

Ack Llewellin kicked off, Bancroft returned and Alun Morgan kicked to touch in the visitors 25. The home forwards, headed by Tom Hemsworth, soon dribbled to the line. Jimmy Lewis then obtained and transferred to Harry Williams, who threw to Ben Tiley and the latter going at top speed scored a try within three minutes of the start amidst tremendous applause, which was renewed when Alun Morgan converted. On the restart Harry Stead got away from a succeeding scrummage in rare style to the centre, where Tom Hemsworth picked up and ran into the visitors 25. Towards halftime, Ross Thomas mulled the ball, and Harry Williams picking up and got away in beautiful fashion to within ten yards of the 25 flag, where he threw to A B Evans and the latter going at top speed scored a fine try. Alun Morgan made a good but unsuccessful attempt at goal, leaving the halftime score Pontypridd one goal and one try to nil.

After lemons, Bancroft restarted for Swansea. Jack Murray in return made a fine run to the centre. Soon Bancroft obtained but could not get very far before he was brought low by Murray. Bancroft again obtained and tried for a drop goal, but only a minor resulted. After the drop-out, play waged in the centre for a considerable time. Eventually a free changed the venue to the home 25. The visiting forwards dribbled to the line and pressed for a while in close proximity. However, the homesters, playing with fourteen men owing to Harry Stead being injured, soon retaliated and brought a fine dribble to the centre. Here, Arnold obtained and kicked to the home 25, and Bancroft, following up well, kicked over the line, but Jack Murray kicked dead. Towards the end, Jimmy Lewis obtained and transferred to Stead, but the pass was ruled forward, and a good chance at scoring was lost, as Harry Stead had no-one to beat. Jack Murray then made a good attempt at a drop goal, but only a minor resulted. After the drop-out the visitors were severely pressed until the end, when Pontypridd emerged the victors by one goal and one try to nil (8-0). A few weeks later at the Pontypridd Football Club AGM the statement of accounts showed that the club had handed over £50 to the Great Western Colliery disaster fund, the proceeds from the two benefit matches.

Review

The season was finally over. The amalgamation of the Pontypridd and Maritime clubs had been a considerable success. The results had been perhaps the best ever, with a playing record unbettered for many decades. The highlight of the season was undoubtedly the win against Swansea at St Helens, while the only minor disappointment was that they were unable to defeat Cardiff at Taff Vale Park, even though defeat was by the narrowest of margins. Since the Pontypridd club had been reconstituted in 1890 the club had scaled heights never before reached and had brought them to the forefront of football in the principality. It was a peak that would rarely be reached by any representatives of the town club, certainly not before the end of the nineteenth century, and possibly not until season 1962-63 when they became unofficial Welsh champions for the first time. As for the rest of the 1890s a firm foundation had been set, but the officials of the ex-Maritime club, with the exception of Dr Howard Davies, quickly left the club, while the Maritime players from the North of England, Harry Stead, Tom Hemsworth etc, slowly returned to their homelands, leaving behind them a successful club that carried happy memories of them. By the end of the 1892-93 season, the title "The Pontypridd Football and Athletic Club" had slowly been forgotten and the club appears to have reverted to its original "Pontypridd Football Club".

Results Season 1892-93

1892

				F	A
Sept 17th	Newport Harriers	Home	Won	38	0
Sept 24th	Llwynypia	Away	Won	19	0
Sept 8th	Llandaff	Home	Won	9	3
Sept 15th	Aberavon	Away	Draw	0	0
Sept 20th	Cardiff	Home	Lost	0	3
Sept 22nd	Penygraig	Home	Draw	3	3
Sept 29th	Morriston	Away	Won	5	0
Nov 3rd	Rhondda District	Home	Won	9	0
Nov 5th	Treorchy	Home	Draw	0	0
Nov 7th	Hull Britannia	Home	Won	3	0
Nov 12th	Llanelly	Home	Lost	0	4
Nov 19th	Neath	Away	Lost	3	5
Nov 26th	Penarth	Away	Draw	0	0
Dec 3rd	Welsh Trial - Taff Vale Park				
Dec 5th	St Davids (Cardiff)	Home	Won	6	0
Dec 10th	Penygraig	Away	Won	3	0
Dec 17th	Pillgwelly (Newport)	Home	Won	11	0
Dec 24th	Wortley	Away	Won	24	3
Dec 26th	Sowerby Bridge	Away	Won	12	3
Dec 27th	Hull Britannia	Away	Won	8	3
Dec 28th	Hunslet	Away	Postponed		

1893

Jan 14th	Cardiff Harlequins	Away	Postponed		
Jan 21st	Llanelly	Away	Lost	0	6
Jan 28th	Llandaff	Home	Won	16	0
Feb 6th	Penygraig	Home	Won	6	0
Feb 11th	Neath	Home	Won	6	0
Feb 18th	Treorchy	Away	Won	6	0
Feb 25th	Aberavon	Home	Draw	3	3
Mar 4th	Cogan	Home	Won	21	0
Mar 6th	Penygraig	Away	Won	5	0
Mar 12th	Treorchy	Home	Won	24	0
Mar 15th	Cardiff	Away	Lost	0	19
Mar 18th	Morriston	Home	Won	10	4
Mar 20th	Swansea	Away	Won	4	3
Mar 25th	Penarth	Home	Won	13	8

Mar 27th	Llwynypia	Home	Won	16	0
Mar 30th	Sowerby Bridge	Home	Postponed		
Apr 1st	Pontardawe	Home	Postponed		
Apr 21st	Newport/Cardiff XV	Home	Lost	6	8
Apr 28th	Swansea/Morriston XV	Home	Won	8	0

The above list is compiled from newspaper reports as no end of season result sheet was produced. The 1893 AGM gave the playing record as follows: Played 37, Won 26, Drawn 6, Lost 5.

Captain first XV, Ack Llewellin/Steve Sullivan; Vice Captain, Alun Morgan; Secretary, Edward Llewellin; Treasurer, S Humphreys; Captain second XV, Benny Lewis; Vice Captain, George Seaton; President, David Leyshon; Vice Presidents, James Roberts + Mr Major Hague; Ground, Taff Vale Park; Headquarters, Victoria Hotel.

The 1892-93 season would long be remembered with affection by the Pontypridd enthusiasts, and for many years was used as a yardstick for end of season records. The following letter appeared in The Glamorgan Free Press of November 1895:

'Dear Sir

It is a matter of surprise that the Pontypridd football team is showing such in and out form of late and it seems a pity that players, after being picked to play, should put the match committee to a lot of bother finding substitutes because of refusals.

I have for my own benefit searched up the record of the team which will long be remembered for all the records it set up during the 1892-93 season. That year, the first XV played less than 22 men the whole season and the players who invariably played in the back division were - Walter Gay, Alun Morgan, Benny Lewis,

Jimmy Green, A B Evans, Jack Murray; while Harry Williams and Jimmy Lewis usually played at half.

If I remember rightly the forwards were also nearly the same eight throughout the season and were - Ack Llewellin, Tom Hemsworth, Harry Stead, Jack Wilkins, Patsy Devereaux, Willie Parkin, Tom Murray and Tom Bryant.

Now, it is not possible to settle down a good team to turn out faithfully for the home games let alone the away games, unless there is consistent selection. For the benefit of the football public I shall give the record for the 1892-93 season, it ought to stimulate the present team to do likewise. Played 37, Won 26, Drew 6, Lost 5. The number of points scored was 318 and those conceded 76, a truly magnificent performance.

Yours Truly
'A Pontypridd Supporter'

Having reached such a peak there was only way that the club could go and that was down, but rather than a steep decline, it was a gradual loss of status over the years, but, as they say "That is another Story!"

The End